2004

Action Research for Inclusive Education

This book presents and discusses an approach to action research which can help dismantle discriminatory and exclusionary practices in education. Insider accounts of action research will help challenge assumptions about the supposed limits of inclusive education, and offer examples of how change can be realistically achieved, through processes of collaboration and participation.

Written by a team of practitioner researchers drawn from a wide range of schools and services, this book provides a groundbreaking guide to action research in inclusive education. The chapters address a wide range of real-life situations and experiences by exploring ways in which teachers have tackled inequalities in the school environment through action research based on principles of equality and democracy. These include:

- the co-ordination of services for minority ethnic groups, including refugee and asylum seeking children;
- peer mediation of access to the literary hour for young children with autism;
- homosexuality and action in the inclusion of gay issues;
- developing the role of learning support assistants in pioneering inclusion;
- reducing exclusion of children with challenging behaviour;
- listening to the voices of young people identified as having severe learning difficulties;
- developing links between special and mainstream schools;
- challenging marginalising practices in Further Education.

Those seeking to empower marginalised individuals and groups through powerful research in action in education will find this book inspiring and engaging. It will be particularly valuable to practitioners, researchers in academic or government settings, student teachers, and those involved in in-service courses and Continuing Professional Development programmes.

Felicity Armstrong is Senior Lecturer in Inclusive Education at the Institute of Education, University of London. **Michele Moore** is Director of the Inclusive Education and Equality Research Centre, University of Sheffield.

Action Research for Inclusive Education

Changing places, changing practice, changing minds

edited by
Felicity Armstrong and
Michele Moore

 RoutledgeFalmer
Taylor & Francis Group

LONDON AND NEW YORK

First published 2004
by RoutledgeFalmer
11 New Fetter Lane, London EC4P 4EE

Simultaneously published in the USA and Canada
by RoutledgeFalmer
29 West 35th Street, New York, NY 10001

RoutledgeFalmer is an imprint of the Taylor & Francis Group

© 2004 Felicity Armstrong and Michele Moore

Typeset in Garamond and Gill Sans by
Florence Production Ltd, Stoodleigh, Devon
Printed and bound in Great Britain by
The Cromwell Press, Trowbridge, Wiltshire

British Library Cataloguing in Publication Data
A catalogue record for this book is available
from the British Library

Library of Congress Cataloging in Publication Data
Action research for inclusive education : changing places,
    changing practice, changing minds / [edited by]
    Felicity Armstrong and Michele Moore.
        p. cm.
        Includes bibliographical references and index.
    1. Inclusive education – Research – Great Britain.   2. Action research
    in education – Great Britain.   3. Educational change – Great Britain.
    I. Armstrong, Felicity.   II. Moore, Michele, 1962–
    LC1203.G7A54 2004
    371.9′046′072–dc22   2003017132

ISBN 0–415–31802–5 (pbk)
ISBN 0–415–31801–7 (hbk)

Contents

Contributors

Felicity Armstrong is a senior lecturer at the Institute of Education, University of London. She teaches on courses relating to inclusive education and her research interests include: policy making and social justice in education; cross-cultural and cross-disciplinary approaches to research; inclusive education; the history and geography of education; practitioner research and the democratisation of research agendas and methodologies.

Kathy Charles works as an educational psychologist in a large city, and has worked as a psychologist and as a mainstream teacher in another LEA. Her interests included the transition from primary to secondary school for children with difficulties related to what are known as 'autistic spectrum disorders'.

Mary Clifton is an Ethnic Minority Achievement Consultant working in an LEA team. This involves supporting schools across the LEA in their development of strategies and policies to address the needs of minority ethnic pupils. She worked for many years in adult education and in schools teaching English as an additional language, and promoting cultural and linguistic inclusion.

Karen Dunn is Head of Applied Studies in Education, Childhood and Counselling at Sheffield Hallam University. She has researched and written extensively in the field of child development, services for families and children and education matters. Her recent research includes developing Parent Partnership, evaluation of Sure Start programmes and best practice in inclusive out-of-school provision and play space.

Judith Gwynn is a teacher in a 'specialist' secondary school in the north of England, having previously taught in a variety of mainstream primary and secondary schools. Her professional and family experiences have stimulated a major interest in inclusive education and community and she is particularly interested in issues concerning identity and empowerment. She is inclusion co-ordinator at her school, where she has carried out research on voice and identities of students described as having 'severe learning difficulties'.

Michele Moore is Director of the Inclusive Education and Equality Research Centre at the University of Sheffield and an executive editor of *Disability and Society*. She has carried out research seeking to advance an agenda for inclusion with disabled people, their families and their representative agencies over many years. She is interested in bridging the gulf between what goes on in the context of academic research and the actuality of the everyday lives of children and those who live or work with them.

Linda Simpson is a Learning Support Co-ordinator at a secondary school in the north of England. She has taught in a number of schools in both the primary and the secondary sectors, and has also worked as an LEA adviser for the Pupil and Support Service.

Colin J. Slater is a teacher whose professional experience in London and Australia has been in a variety of educational institutions, including nursery settings, mainstream primary schools, adult colleges, hospital schools and special units for pupils identified as having special educational needs.

Catherine Sorsby is a teacher in a primary school with an Integrated Resource Unit for children labelled as having 'special educational needs'. She is always keen to extend the range of experiences and opportunities available to others, whether children or adults. Cath recognises the difficulties associated with inclusive education in the UK but is optimistic that it will be more successful than the present education system.

Val Thompson is Inclusive Learning Co-ordinator at a large College of Further Education in the Midlands. She has worked in FE for sixteen years and prior to that as a local authority advisory teacher in secondary schools.

Pauline Zelaieta is a teacher in charge of an Inclusion Team, working from within a school designated for children identified as having severe, complex and profound learning difficulties, aged 2–11 years. She has worked for many years to overcome barriers to inclusion, and her enthusiastic involvement in developing a collaborative and supportive role for special schools and increasing learning opportunities for all have been at the core of her working practices.

Foreword

Len Barton

Having a desire to learn more about the perspectives and experiences of teachers in the increasingly complex, diverse and changing world of schools and post-school institutions, I approached reading this collection of insider accounts with an eager anticipation. I was not disappointed. Overall, the chapters contain a wealth of careful reflections, examples of critical incidents and significant challenges, of frustrations and uncertainties, points of risk-taking as well as new understandings and a clear indication of the fundamental importance of how these teachers viewed teaching in terms of making a difference in the lives of their pupils.

Inclusive thinking and practice are hard work and this is exemplified through insights into some of the complexities and contradictory contexts in which their teaching and research took place. It is also reflected in the serious questions that are raised in these accounts. Overall, the book is an informative, thoughtful, stimulating read. In the foreword I will identify several factors that have impressed me and which I feel are important to highlight. These are not meant to be exhaustive nor are they presented in order of priority.

An important dimension of the writing concerns the openness and honesty of these teachers. They express some of their deeply felt views about the ambiguity and contradictory nature of the national and local policy directives and contexts, the varied challenges that they had to continually face in their work, the personal and professional dilemmas and compromises that are a feature of their experiences as well as self-critical analysis of aspects of their practice. These chapters do therefore reflect the contradictions and messiness of the real world in which these teachers daily work and struggle.

Another impressive feature concerns the range and challenging nature of the questions that are raised, including those that are focused on their own personal and professional assumptions, values and understandings. These demonstrate the seriousness of their reflections with regard to identifying and challenging the varied barriers to learning and participation and establishing a series of priorities and agendas for future engagement. The

motivation for this practice is the desire to realise a more effective relationship between their developing understanding of inclusive ideas and
values and their daily classroom teaching. Part of this learning process, as
their accounts demonstrate, involves disturbing elements of confusion, doubt
and the importance of acknowledging what they cannot do on their own.
The centrality of working towards whole-school/college approaches to
the pursuit of change is another encouraging message derived from these
accounts.

A further impression derived from the reading of these chapters is the
vivid sense of the passion and commitment that these teachers express
towards their work and especially to the pursuit of change. The time, energy,
emotionality and thoughtfulness involved in their work and their relationships with pupils and colleagues demonstrate the importance of the position
and role of teachers in the implementation of policy. The examples of sensitive observations, interpretations and interventions, the exercise of creative
and imaginative thinking, the process of risk-taking and learning from
mistakes, all testify to the quality and degree of the resolution underpinning their practice. This is being achieved against and from within the
constraints of a highly selective and divisive educational system which
provides the barriers to inclusive relationships and participation for all
learners.

These chapters provide support for confirming that there are no simple
blueprints or slick, quick solutions to the task of inclusive thinking, relations and practice. They also remind the reader that there is no room for
complacency in the pursuit of understanding, and implementing, the contribution education can make to maximising the participation of all learners
and the removal of discriminatory and exclusionary assumptions and practices. They also point to the importance of exploring and understanding
these factors within particular contexts.

A final aspect of the book concerns the ways in which the contributors
have drawn on some principles from action research, to explore a range of
fascinating and professionally relevant topics in order to develop a more
critically informed understanding that is connected with the pursuit of
change. The topics of research include: pupils at risk of exclusion; the partnership between colleagues in special and mainstream education; the position
and experiences of learning support staff, research through collaboration
with a disabled individual, the position of a learning support unit; the
voices and experiences of students who experience exclusion as a result of
attitudes and practices relating to cultural and linguistic difference; insider
perceptions of four disabled teenagers and the issue of gay students and
inclusive education.

The teachers have approached their projects as part of an interpretative
activity that attempts to make particular aspects of decision making in relation to the planning, development of research question(s), the process of

the project and outcomes, transparent. Thus research is viewed as a learning process with issues of accountability and ethics being an important feature of this form of investigation. The conception of research is complex and dynamic, involving recognition of the realities of uncertainty and lack of predictability within the research practice. The researcher is involved in negotiating and consulting over the meaning and practice of such key factors as 'planning', 'implementation' and 'dissemination'. This form of practice entails engaging with contradictory and controversial issues in which unexpected questions emerge, or, more appropriately, are thrown up. Central to quality research of this nature is the art of listening to unfamiliar voices or of listening to familiar ones in new ways. This raises the possibility of questioning the inappropriate use of specific categories as reflecting the real abilities of the participants. In seeking to contribute to the development of inclusive policies and practices the research process entails a strong emphasis on collaborative power and effort and the centrality of respect and trust in the establishment of collegial relationships.

Thinking about the chapters as a whole has enabled me to identify some important impressions. These have been overwhelmingly positive. This is not to say I have no disagreements about particular interpretations or ideas that are offered in specific papers. Nor am I implying that there is no difference between some of the papers in terms of levels of detail and analysis. What is clear to me is that I have benefited from thinking about the chapters as a whole. They have provided me with questions, insights and examples that I need to think more about and in different ways.

Producing an edited collection of papers is not as easy as some people may assume. This is especially true of this collection in that most contributors are writing for publication for the first time. I am grateful that the editors saw the project through to completion and it has now become a published work. Thanks also to the teachers. I am confident that I will not be the only one who has found reading the chapters to be an informative and thought-provoking experience.

Len Barton
Professor of Inclusive Education
Institute of Education
University of London

Chapter 1

Action research

Developing inclusive practice and transforming cultures

Felicity Armstrong and Michele Moore

In this chapter we explore the nature of practitioner research in relation to issues of exclusion and inclusion in education. We look briefly at 'classic' approaches to action research and then reflect on how these may be adapted, stretched, re-formed and used by practitioners to develop research projects which explicitly seek to advance an agenda for inclusion through the research process itself, as well as by bringing about changes to institutional cultures and practices. We provide some possible guidelines for approaching action research that can be used by practitioners and their co-researchers, or which can be simply explored as a means of raising questions or for understanding contexts and situations from a number of different perspectives. We have found in our own work that a multitude of controversies, confusions and contradictions are uncovered during the research process which touch on issues relating to inclusion and exclusion, so that whereas 'action research' *is* a central theme throughout our work, and embedded in the projects described in this book, we have a shared feeling that we are mapping the power of 'research action' as we struggle with the parameters of action research as classically defined. Suggestions we make are built out of our own assorted research experience, or borrowed from those of other researchers and practitioners, and are not intended as 'rules' which must be rigidly followed. 'Models' can quickly become straitjackets if they are not seen as subject to constant renegotiation and interpretation. The contributions in this book reflect these tensions and should not, therefore, be seen as prescriptive or examples of 'ideal practice', but they may be useful as a starting point for reflection and further research. A major purpose of the book is to encourage practitioners in bringing about change in their own work contexts through research action which, of necessity, will be idiosyncratic and characterised by internal variability, but which will begin to develop credible approaches and resources for inspiring and initiating change. The chapters which make up this book are examples of the breadth of issues which can be explored through practitioner research, and highlight some of the unexpected issues and outcomes which may emerge in the research process.

Action research, in the context of this chapter and the other contributions in the book, is used as a general term to describe processes of planning, transformation and evaluation which draw on insider practitioner enquiry and reflection and which focus on reducing inequalities and exclusion in education. We are particularly interested in the possibilities which may be opened up for bringing about change in local contexts by those who are closely connected with them. We see action research – or 'research action' – as, potentially, an approach in which a transfer of power takes place from those who, in the context of the relationship between research departments, government agencies and schools, have traditionally carried out research to those who have historically been on the receiving end of change planned and imposed by outside agencies. As we move through the chapter we look at questions relating to voice and empowerment and suggest some possible relationships between these and democratic research action.

The term 'action research' refers to the cyclical nature of collaborative planning, carrying out the evaluation of a particular intervention which has an identifiable focus and purpose, but which does not predetermine outcomes, or discard those that are unexpected. At the same time we recognise the complexity of social settings such as schools and colleges, and the artificial nature of identifying a 'focus' as if it were possible to delineate a bounded area of social life without taking into account the dynamic and reciprocal relationships between contexts. When we refer to a research *focus* we understand that this is a social construction and one that is likely to be disturbed and challenged in the research process. Action research generates knowledge, as well as being concerned with bringing about change, through processes of observation, reflection and critical engagement with ideas and practices. A project which does not appear to have been 'successful' in terms of achieving its original purposes may be highly productive in terms of raising fresh issues and challenging previous assumptions and theories. We do not separate what might be regarded as 'instrumental' agendas of action research from the production of knowledge.

We use the term 'research action' to include all research-based activity which engages with the day-to-day life of institutions with the purpose of bringing about change. At times, we use this term and 'action research' almost interchangeably.

Practitioner research and the political economy of knowledge production

In recent years there has been a drive from government and some university departments to ensure that research in education is linked with the implementation of government policy, particularly as part of a wider agenda concerned with 'school improvement' and 'raising standards'. This concern has led to a number of government initiatives through the different branches of the

Department for Education and Skills (DFES), such as the DfES Best Practice Research Scholarship scheme in which teachers receive funding to carry out a piece of research, supported by a 'mentor', designed to improve practice and raise levels of attainment. The General Teaching Council for England (GTC) is committed to transforming teaching into an 'evidenced-based profession' in which teachers are identified as playing a key role in 'shaping the development of professional policy and practice to maintain and set professional standards' (GTC Web site, 2003), and aims to support a closer relationship between research and practitioners. The Centre for Using Research and Evidence in Education (CUREE) is a body contracted by the DfES to 'identify research and quality assure it with particular consumers in mind' and 'Each topic is presented and structured according to a series of questions that the GTC has designed to bring out the message for teachers and teaching.' The DfES held its first annual research conference in 2001 during which practitioners presented their research, and the Teacher Training Agency (TTA) has organised a number of initiatives such as school-based research consortia and national conferences. In order to ensure that government messages concerning policy and 'good practice' reach all teachers, the DfES launched *Teachers' Magazine* in 1999, 230,000 copies of which are sent direct to teachers' homes.

The relationship between research and practitioners as conceptualised by the DfES is clearly related to 'the political economy of knowledge production' (Noffke, 2002) in support of government policies and values. Research carried out by teachers, linked with government initiatives of the kinds described above, is harnessed to particular government agendas such as 'raising attainment' and, in this sense, practitioners' research is 'politicised'. This does not mean, of course, that individual teachers who become involved in government-sponsored practitioner research become passive instruments of government policy. Some of the contributions in this book are based on initial work carried out as part of DfES Best Practice Research projects, which have been used as starting points for innovative research and which explore quite different agendas from those concerned with narrow interpretations of 'raising attainment'. Focusing on inclusion issues inevitably transforms the nature of the debate.

Action research may also be highly politicised in a very different way as a form of contestation or resistance in which, through the process of exploration and discovery, old issues are reconfigured and unexpected questions emerge. This disturbance, this movement, which is generated through the research process involving new collaborations and the creation of arenas in which democratic debate takes place, may be profoundly challenging to the status quo. Practitioner researchers may meet with passivity, non-compliance or hostility on the part of other teachers or senior management. In our experience, projects which are based on a premise of consultation and participation can facilitate new conditions for research in which platforms for resistance are established.

At the micro-level, Noffke (2002) explains two contrasting purposes of action research in terms of the 'expected outcomes of the research process',

> To some working in action research, *its goal has been represented as lying primarily within the areas of personal/and or professional development*. Action research, in this way, is valued less for its role in the production of knowledge about curriculum, pedagogy, and the social contexts of schools, and more for its ability to help teachers 'grow' in their self-awareness in terms of their professional skills and dispositions. This is clearly an important 'potential'. Yet . . . a sole emphasis in this area not only misses important aspects to the work of education, *it can provide an avenue for the 'social engineering' of particular attitudes and dispositions* among teachers to the exclusion of others, primarily the focus on technical questions of 'delivery' to the exclusion of questions of curriculum and social justice.
>
> (Noffke, 2002, p. 20, our italics)

The work underpinning the different chapters in this book is very much concerned with exploring possibilities at different levels and these include transforming our own research practice as part of a wider agenda for advancing social justice, as well as bringing about transformation at institutional, attitudinal and practice-based levels.

Action research and democracy

Action research has been used as a means of *imposing* policy change and of *implementing* policy (sometimes no more than a 'gentler' version of imposing change). In contrast, it has also been interpreted as an approach to research which *challenges* top-down policy making and hegemonically imposed values, and it can be used as a powerful mechanism for transforming school cultures and empowering schools, teachers and pupils. In this sense, action research may provide an arena in which struggles take place over values, meanings and practice. It is potentially powerful both as a technical instrument for introducing, monitoring and evaluating change involving small or large institutions and groups of people, and as a vehicle for social and cultural transformation in which principles, practices and values are examined, and discussion, negotiation and reflection go on all the time.

In talking about 'action research' we do not have in mind a set of instructions or technical requirements; rather, we refer to a fluid approach, involving an exploration of values and practices in which the focal participants are the main agents for changing the environments in which they are situated and consultation and collaboration are key element in the research design and process.

Consultation may be extended to all members of an actual or prospective research community, in particular children and young people, including those who are differently articulate, as well as teachers, parents, policy makers and other key stakeholders. We are advocating the kind of approach to research which aims not to do things *to* people, but to build a shared and democratic approach to transformation involving everyone. We feel strongly that the agenda for positive social change should not be confined to the researcher's own preoccupations, but must be looked for in the starting points and aspirations of those for whom the research is primarily concerned by listening to their voices. But already we are running into difficulties, because what primarily distinguishes principles of inclusion from, for example, 'integration', is that all members of the community are concerned and implicated by all exclusions and by every step taken towards greater inclusion. By identifying and naming a particular group as 'vulnerable' or 'at risk of exclusion' we may, implicitly, be contributing to the construction of an identity of 'the excluded other'. We are acutely aware of this difficulty, and have tried to overcome it by resisting the use of labels and by making connections between the many levels of exclusion which take place in education. This is reflected in the diversity of material in the chapters of this book, although we cannot claim to have eliminated all forms of marginalising discourses in our own practice either as researchers or editors.

In the process of editing the book we have become sensitive to the apparent ease with which it is possible to adopt uncritically terminology used in familiar contexts, and even contribute to the invention of new exclusionary labels and stereotypes ourselves. We have had many discussions about this with different contributors, particularly in relation to the use of labels and categories which are embedded in their daily work contexts and practices. This is an important issue because the language used to discuss and write about research is, we believe, an integral part of the research process itself in which values and identity-making practices, and processes of marginalisation and exclusion, are potentially as *real*, as *powerful* and as *pervasive* as they are in the daily interactions that take place in schools, colleges and policy-making arenas.

In the context of participatory action research, based on emancipatory principles, all those who are implicated in change would participate in identifying and planning that change, and monitoring and evaluating it, planning the next stage, and so on. However, in the context of education, this presupposes a very high level of democracy in settings in which students' voices are clearly audible and valued. We have found that this presents real challenges in terms of attempting to adopt democratic practices in *unde*-mocratic environments (and these include our *own* habits and patterns of thinking and behaving). For this reason, we see our work, and the projects discussed in the different chapters of this book, as just a beginning in terms of challenging exclusionary systems, values and practices. The difficulties we have encountered, in terms of bringing about change and in involving people who are more usually positioned as recipients of policy changes, have led to a critical engagement with deeply rooted assumptions and ideas (Armstrong, 2003; Goodley and Moore, 2000, 2002). This process has been akin to what Freire (1973), writing of social change, has described in the following terms:

> a society beginning to move from one epoch to another requires the development of an especially flexible, critical spirit. Lacking such a spirit, men [*and women*] cannot perceive the marked contradictions which occur in society as emerging values in search of affirmation and fulfilment clash with earlier values seeking self-preservation.
>
> (Freire, 1973, p. 7)

Attempts to develop inclusive education through practitioner research, in a period in which education has become profoundly commodified and competitive, and processes of selection have become intensified, inevitably lead to conflict between different sets of values and goals. But it is at the points of confrontation that new perspectives on existing arrangements and taken-for-granted cultures and practices emerge, and new questions are raised. In this sense, critical research action on the part of practitioners is powerful in generating ideas and fresh theoretical perspectives.

In the following sections we provide some possible starting points for those of you who are embarking on action research in your own schools or other work contexts. Again, we want to stress that these are 'suggestions', and open to interpretation, negotiation and rejection in favour of approaches which you find more useful to the particular issues you are facing. We comment on some of the adaptations we have made to the classic action research approach to show how inclusivity and empowerment can be maximised within research practice as well as through research outcomes.

Changing practice through action research: starting out

There are a number of tasks which face practitioner researchers as they set out to develop greater understanding of the range of conditions, principles and practices which are involved in bringing about change in support of developing inclusive education. Broadly speaking, initial preparatory work may typically include:

- Reading some of the key literature in the area, including policy documents relating to policy making at national, LEA and school level which relate to, or have an impact on, equality issues in education and developing a critical approach to reading. At this stage it will be helpful and stimulating to search out kinds of writing and documents which, perhaps, go against the main stream of thinking, or suggest radical alternatives to normative positions. The *Index for Inclusion* (Booth *et al.*, 2002) is one such document in that it suggests a radical whole-school and community approach for transforming schools.

- Beginning to use a research notebook, or 'diary' from the outset, in which you write down ideas, quotations, questions and observations.
- Broadening your understanding and, with others, raising critical questions concerning pedagogy and curriculum and school or college culture through an exploration of different teaching and learning contexts.
- Developing an understanding of the principles and practices of practitioner research as a means of exploring the culture and values underpinning your own institutions as they translate into practice.
- Building relationships with others and creating arenas in which issues and projects can be discussed (or bringing these issues and projects to existing arenas).
- Beginning to identify an area of particular concern and interest for your research focus.
- Constantly reflecting on the issues raised through these activities in the light of principles of equality and rights.

The initial challenge is to draw together and translate these activities into a focused, manageable piece of research which increases understanding about the barriers to inclusion and challenges exclusionary practices, and in which collaboration with others is possible. Indeed, we would be misrepresenting the role of researchers if we suggested that they should work through these challenges alone. Practitioner-researchers belong to communities whose members have much to offer in terms of providing support, collaboration, information and a range of different perspectives on familiar and unfamiliar issues. Others, such as students, support workers, colleagues and managers are inevitably drawn into the research experience and all have expert knowledge to contribute. Understanding how these others are positioned in relation to proposed research can help to shape the enquiry and dramatically influence the relevance and power of any project. For this reason we have changed our own perspectives on the importance of collaboration with others as part of creating inclusive practices through the research process itself. We now position consultation as the critical starting point. If possible, we want our research to be perceived as valuable, relevant and useful by those on the receiving end of, or affected by, research outcomes, and we want our concerns and purposes to be ones they prioritise themselves.

An important early stage in an action research project is the setting up of a small group which will work with you on all stages of the project – this might include another teacher, a teaching assistant, a group of children, groups who experience exclusion or discrimination or who want to explore these issues in the wider context of their school or college. Inevitably, in many cases there will be a lead researcher or co-ordinator.

Tasks which face you and the group include:

- Discussing and negotiating necessary permissions to carry out your project.
- Identifying possible constraints or opportunities which may present themselves in the course of carrying out your research.
- Designing your methodology. How are you going to carry out your project? How will you monitor it and evaluate it?
- Thinking in advance about the analytical tools to be used to try and make sense of the research process and outcomes.
- Drawing up a timetable.
- Planning a dissemination strategy – which can be built in to the research process – in order to maximise the impact of the work.

All these activities become easier to follow through if consultation is optimised. For example, uncertainty about the focus of the work can be addressed through discussion with key stakeholders; tensions around access to research participants can be reduced if gatekeepers have a meaningful say in what you are going to do. The chances of the analysis being seen as 'wrong' or of your final report being dismissed as 'irrelevant' are greatly reduced if those implicated in, or affected by, the work are kept in the consultation loop. It would be misleading, however, to imply the process of consultation invariably runs smoothly. That it does not has been plainly documented in our writing elsewhere (Moore *et al.*, 1998, Moore and Dunn, 1999). But research which is not based on a premise of consultation has frequently been described as 'a waste of time' (Oliver, 1992, 1997). Thus we know ourselves to be researching in a theoretical, methodological and practical framework of struggle in which *consultation and collaboration* are pivotal but not unproblematic.

During the course of any research activity, it is helpful to keep grappling with questions such as 'Why am I doing *this* project rather than something else?' 'In whose interests is this project?' 'What connection has it with developing inclusive cultures and practices?' 'Is it actually possible to plan, carry out and evaluate this project in the time available?' 'Am I consulting others involved as far as I reasonably can?' 'How does this work fit in to the overall policy, culture and existing practices of the school or local education authority (where appropriate) or other focal institution or agency?' 'Does it actually challenge existing practices which shore up exclusions and if so, what are the implications?'

As suggested above, a practice that will be helpful as well as challenging at times will be keeping a record of reflections and processes in the form of a diary or journal. 'What difference is the research making?' is a question to which you should constantly return – throughout the research process as well as when considering its eventual uses.

Theories and beliefs

One purpose of practitioner research is to support the generation of theory, in the sense that the processes and changes which emerge through your project may have an impact on the way you – and others – understand other theories, ideas, beliefs and practices. As soon as you have decided the focus of your enquiry you have begun to identify your theoretical interest. The question of what you will end up researching, like that of why you are doing your research, throws the matter of objectivity versus subjectivity into sharp relief and exposes a large part of the methodological struggle which researchers in all kinds of social justice research face. The answers to these questions reveal that even before you start you have a partisan position. We can draw on some of our own ongoing projects to illustrate this point. For example, we are interested in finding out about young people's experiences of permanent exclusion *because we feel this will help elucidate strategies for keeping these students in the same settings as their peers;* we are interested in evaluating parent partnership projects *because we would like to push local authorities to improve their support of families whose children have impairments;* we are using research evaluation as a tool to develop good practice guidance on accessible play space *because we want disabled children to have the same opportunities of the social experience of play as their non-disabled siblings and peers;* we are researching the literal and symbolic use of space in the schools and communities *so that we can understand more about the different means and levels through which exclusions take place so that these can be challenged.* Our work seeks to optimise the relationship between research practice, an agenda for inclusion and the everyday contexts in which inclusions and exclusions are played out. It is fundamentally antithetical to the possibility of objectivity in respect of this commitment. We have many vested interests, and that is why we place emphasis on consultation with insiders to inform and check the elaboration of our theoretical discourses and to offer alternative perspectives and guidance.

The traditional tendency in research is to try to ignore or minimise the influence of insider perspectives and to establish distance between a researcher's own commitments and the context in which research is carried out. But for practitioner-researchers this expectation poses problems in a number of respects. First, in the context of researching for inclusive education, practitioner-researchers are often trying to make sense of their own practices and work contexts as well as interpreting cultures and practices that are far from their own. Second, experienced practitioners who are willing to reconceptualise their own working practices through the medium of research will have formulated questions out of a deep and intimate interest in the situation they are proposing to study. Practitioner-researchers are not independent surveyors with no preconceived ideas, rather they are well informed with ideas forged through day-to-day close-up observation of complex social practices and competing pressures. They have suspicions and hunches about research issues that, we argue, should not be minimised or left out of the picture. Critics will always be able to dispute whether you have presented the 'real picture', but arguably this position is based on a false premise that there is one objective account, only one 'reality', possible. Practitioner research which seeks to reduce inequalities can be partial, it can be disturbing and messy, it can raise more questions than it answers, it is always contingent, provisional and ideological, and it is based on commitment to changing power relations in order to advance an agenda for inclusion. It is – as far as possible – informed by the perspectives of those who experience marginalisation and oppression, and those who are working in contexts in which they themselves are closely linked with issues and practices relating to inclusion and exclusion.

Whether the accounts presented can be regarded as 'reliable' or 'valid' depends on beliefs about objectivity. *Our* belief is that *all* research is political in the sense that it is always concerned with, or undertaken to further, *someone's* interests; it is *never* value-free. But by fixing the origins of the research firmly to a premise of consultation and collaboration with those for whom the research is most closely concerned we can move some considerable way to reducing the risk that the research will be exploitative, well intentioned but wrong-footed or even injurious. Good research planning involves recognising the sources of bias which surround the way you are going to formulate your study and facing up to many complex questions about the meaning of a neutral or, conversely, biased, stance as part of the struggle for change through action research. We are advocating a position which accepts that there are different ways of viewing the world and that the conclusions you arrive at will be very much the product of multiple, negotiated realities. However, although we would argue that values and social practices can 'only be understood within the framework of particular spaces and their cultures at particular times' (Armstrong, 2003, p. 114) we would totally eschew an entirely relativist position in which *all* positions are considered equally acceptable.

Ways of researching

Useful questions to keep coming back to during the research process include: what do you notice about what you are interested in noticing? Should you rethink what you think the research is about? How can you monitor the perceived value of your work? There is a sense of endless reflexivity and the aim is not to go endlessly on and on, but to try to make explicit as much as possible about the parameters within which you are framing your interpretations and subsequent arguments. Clearly articulating the boundaries and limitations of a project helps to define it. Researchers who acknowledge their own starting points are less likely to overstate their claims and recommendations.

It is important to recognise that you may not achieve what you set out to do in your project, but the process of trying and even, perhaps, failing to carry out research can yield as many insights into issues relating to the possibilities and barriers relating to inclusion as a project which appears to bring about a desired change directly. There may also be unexpected outcomes of your action research, which should be noted and considered. In this sense, the project will enable you to 'theorise' about your own practice and work context in a number of ways. Again, your research diary is a good place to try out and develop insights and theories which you will be able to discuss in relation to the work of others, based on your reading. A critical friend is a great asset to any researcher, but do record your ongoing dialogue for future reference.

Those 'working in the field' sometimes experience frustration and feelings of disconnectedness when they read academic books and articles which appear to impose ('from above' as it were) particular rules and jargon relating to research. As Dodds and Hart (2001) write, about their own experience,

> We had both observed that the more mainstream traditional research approaches do not always suit the needs and available resources of practitioner researchers.
>
> The message that some practitioners seemed to receive was that the expertise required for research is qualitatively different from the expertise acquired through practical experience of teaching. When carrying out their own enquiries, some would set aside their own sophisticated, analytical and interpretative expertise, only to find themselves less able to think so effectively through the unfamiliar medium of 'research methods'.
>
> (Dodds and Hart, 2001, p. 7)

As we have started to say, action research, in contrast to other more traditional research methodologies, actually *relies* on the 'analytical and interpretative' expertise of the teacher-researcher in terms of research design, implementation and evaluation. However, this is not to suggest some kind of binary opposition between action research and other research approaches. Action research can draw on a range of methodologies and research tools and may be used in many contexts by all kinds of researchers working together. Neither should it be seen as being concerned entirely with practice and the instrumental pursuit of change; on the contrary, it can be a powerful mechanism through which theories are challenged and developed. It provides a useful framework through which you can maximise the impact of research and theoretical development on practice and in the lives of people who are routinely marginalised and in the lives of those who are seen as not in need of any particular affirmative attention. Inclusive education is *not* about identifying an 'excluded group' and fixing their situation so that they are, in appearance at least, less excluded. Ultimately it is about transforming cultures and practices as they involve, and affect, all members of a community. That is the goal, and that is why the Index for Inclusion (Booth *et al.*, 2002) is potentially such a powerful tool, in that it explains the need for very fundamental and wide reaching change, involving everybody.

Action research can take many different forms but there are a number of features that distinguish it from other kinds of research. Not all these features will necessarily be present in every action research project. Richard Winter (1996) suggests the following as distinguishing characteristics as 'central to the action research process'

- *Reflexive critique*, which is the process of becoming aware of our own perceptual biases,
- *Dialectic critique*, which is a way of understanding the relationship between the various aspects in our own work context,
- *Collaboration*, which is intended to mean that everyone's view is taken as a contribution to understanding the situation,
- *Risking disturbance*, which is an understanding of our own taken-for-granted processes and willingness to submit them to critique,
- *Creating plural structures*, which involves developing various accounts and critiques, rather than a single authoritative interpretation,
- *Theory and practice internalised*, which is seeing theory and practice as two interdependent yet complimentary phases of the change process.

(Winter, in Zuber-Skerritt, 1996, pp. 13–14)

These features clearly imply critically appraising existing structures and practices and values as they impact on particular areas of work and, in particular, the focus of your enquiry.

The process of inclusive action research

Action research has often been described as a *research spiral*, to reflect the cyclical character of its approach. This has been represented diagrammatically in a number of different ways by numerous researchers (e.g., Elliot, 1981, 1992; Kemmis, 1982; Dicks, 2002). Alternative action research spirals depict the 'action – critical reflection – planning' dynamic in different ways. Our variation of the action research spiral (Figure 1.1) explicitly seeks to encourage inclusive processes which advance inclusion through research design, practice and process, and research outcomes. It should not be taken as blueprint for your own research design, but may provide an outline of the kind of structure you wish to develop.

In tracing the different aspects of the research spiral we can see how the different characteristics relate to each other. We hesitate to refer to 'stages'

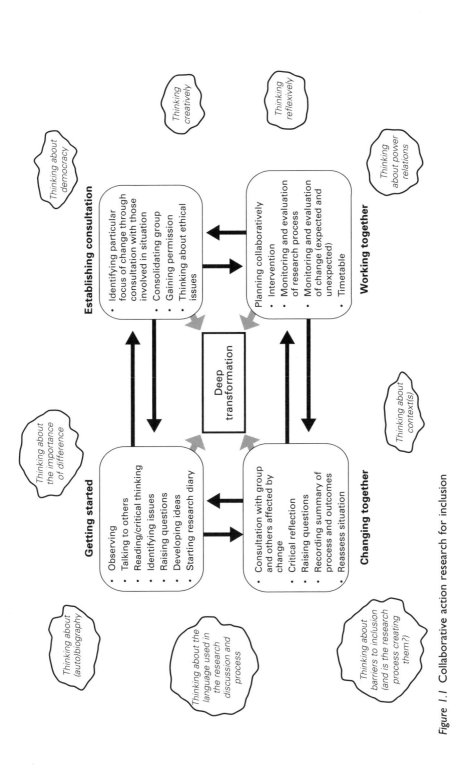

Getting started

- Observing
- Talking to others
- Reading/critical thinking
- Identifying issues
- Raising questions
- Developing ideas
- Starting research diary

Establishing consultation

- Identifying particular focus of change through consultation with those involved in situation
- Consolidating group
- Gaining permission
- Thinking about ethical issues

Changing together

- Consultation with group and others affected by change
- Critical reflection
- Raising questions
- Recording summary of process and outcomes
- Reassess situation

Working together

- Planning collaboratively
- Intervention
- Monitoring and evaluation of research process
- Monitoring and evaluation of change (expected and unexpected)
- Timetable

Deep transformation

Thinking about democracy

Thinking creatively

Thinking reflexively

Thinking about power relations

Thinking about the importance of difference

Thinking about context(s)

Thinking about (auto)biography

Thinking about the language used in the research discussion and process

Thinking about barriers to inclusion (and is the research process creating them?)

Figure 1.1 Collaborative action research for inclusion

– although there *are* some clearly identifiable stages – because this suggests a sequence of segmented activities rather than a continuous, overlapping process of reflection, consultation, planning and change.

The headings and ideas in this diagram relate to the discussion and suggestions already set out in this chapter. You may want to experiment with this spiral in different ways, so we have appended a 'blank' version at the end of the book, which can be photocopied.

Working with the inclusive action research agenda

We have begun to explore some principles and practices of action research in order to suggest a possible framework for your thinking and planning. However, this 'framework' should be elastic and permeable and should not act as a rigid structure which constrains creative exploration. We are thus encouraging you to reinterpret it and develop your own research approach, reflecting the culture, constraints and possibilities presented in your own work context.

The approach we are promoting sets out to democratise the research process through recognising the rights of those whom our research is about. It involves fundamentally valuing the perspective of those who experience exclusion, either because they are themselves excluded or because they are witnessing, producing or seeking to challenge exclusion in whatever form it takes in education – or all these. We are keen that action research in – and for – inclusive education should bridge the gulf between the academic world of research on inclusion and the actuality of people's everyday lives by emphasising that it is those living and working with, and within, the structures, values, practices and political states of play which produce or reduce exclusion in particular settings who best know the questions and issues with which researchers should be concerned and who will have the most productive ideas about how the research process can best be managed. Our overarching intention is to encourage the development of a dynamic reciprocity between research and applied settings in order to advance the project of inclusion, through which fresh perspectives and meanings and creative energy and action can emerge.

We present this discussion of transformative action research, and the accounts of practitioner research which follow in this book, as offering a range of ideas about how exclusion can be challenged through consultation and collaborative action and reflection. You will find the suggestions we have made for inclusive research practice in this chapter are interpreted in a number of different ways in the diverse arenas in which the contributors have set about trying to initiate change.

Some of the research projects presented have not gone as far as others in seeking out the views of others, and few – if any – have really managed to share control of the research focus, planning, process and evaluation with a wider group of people who experience exclusion in some form or another. However, we hope that this discussion, and the experiences and reflections presented in the different chapters will provide you with ideas and inspiration about how you might begin to set about changing places, changing practices and changing minds in relation to your own work context.

References

Armstrong, F. (1999) 'Inclusion, curriculum and the struggle for space in school', *International Journal of Inclusive Education'* 3 (1), 75–87.

Armstrong, F. (2003) *Spaced Out: Policy, Difference and the Challenge of Inclusive Education*, Dordrecht: Kluwer.

Bassey, M. (1992) 'Creating education through research', *British Educational Research Journal* 18 (1), 3–16.

Booth, T., Ainscow, M., Black-Hawkins, K., Vaughn, M. and Shaw, L. (2002) *Index for Inclusion*, Bristol: Centre for Studies on Inclusive Education.

Dicks, B. (2002) *Grounded theory: a thumbnail sketch* (on line). Available at www.scu.edu.au/schools/gcm/ar/arp/grounded.html.

Dodds, M. and Hart, S. (2001) *Doing Practitioner Research Differently*, London: RoutledgeFalmer.

Elliot, J. (1981) *Action Research: A Framework for Self-evaluation in Schools*, TIQL Working Paper No. 1, Cambridge: Cambridge Institute of Education.

Elliot, J. (1992) *Action Research for Educational Change*, Milton Keynes: Open University Press.

Freire, P. (1973) *Education: The Practice of Freedom,* London: Writers' and Readers' Publishing Co-operative.

Goodley, D. and Moore, M. (2000) 'Doing disability research: activist lives and the academy', *Disability and Society* 15 (6), 861–82.

Goodley, D. and Moore, M. (2002) *Arts against Disablement: People with Learning Difficulties and the Performing Arts*, Kidderminster: British Institute of Learning Disabilities Press.

Kemmis, S. and McTaggart, R. (1982) *The Action Research Planner*, Geelong VIC: Deakin University.

Moore, M. and Dunn, K. (1999) Disability, 'human rights and education in Romania', in F. Armstrong and L. Barton (eds) *Disability, Human Rights and Education: Cross-cultural Perspectives*, Buckingham: Open University Press, pp. 193–209.

Noffke, Susan E. (2002) 'Conceptualisations of action research', in C. Day, J. Elliot, B. Somekh, and R. Winter (eds) *Theory and Practice in Action Research*, Wallingford: Symposium Books.

Oliver, M. (1992) 'Changing the social relations of research production', *Disability, Handicap and Society* 7 (2), 101–15.

Oliver, M. (1997) 'Emancipatory research: realistic goal or impossible dream?' in C. Barnes and G. Mercer (eds) *Doing Disability Research*, Leeds: Disability Press.

Stenhouse, L. (1980) *Curriculum Research and Development*, London: Heinemann.

Winter, R. (1996) 'Some principles and procedures for the conduct of action research', in O. Zuber-Skerritt (ed.) *New Directions of Action Research*, London: Falmer Press.

Web sites

General Teaching Council for England www.gtce.org.uk/gtcinfo.asp>
Teachers' Magazine (DfES) www.teachernet.gov.uk>

Further reading

Atweh, B., Kemmis, S. and Weeks, P. (eds) (1998) *Action Research in Practice*, London: Routledge.

Carr, W. and Kemmis, S. (1986) *Becoming Critical: Education, Knowledge and Action Research*, Lewes: Falmer Press.

Dicks, B. (2002) *Action research: action and research* (on line). Available at www.scu.edu.au/schools/gcm/ar/arp/aandr.html.

Gomm, R. and Woods, P. (eds) (1993) *Educational Research in Action*, II, London: Paul Chapman.

Hustler, D., Cassidy, T. and Cuff, T. (eds) (1986) *Action Research in Classrooms and Schools*, London: Allen & Unwin.

Rose, R. and Grosvenor, I. (eds) (2001) *Doing Research in Special Education: Ideas into Practice*, London: David Fulton.

Tilstone, C. (ed.) (1998) *Observing Teaching and Learning: Principles and Practice*, London: David Fulton.

Vulliamy, G. and Webb, R. (eds) (1992) *Teacher Research and Special Educational Needs*, London: David Fulton.

Zuber-Skerritt, O. (ed.) (1996) *New Directions of Action Research*, London: Falmer Press.

Chapter 2

Disability and empowerment

Personal integrity in further education research

Val Thompson

This chapter describes an action research project that developed from consultation with a disabled learner. The project attempted to work to established principles in joint, participative research action and to examine some difficult questions that surfaced. These questions, which have to do with personal and professional relationships, prejudice and power, are discussed because they shed light on the complexity of maintaining personal integrity in research which explicitly sets out to contribute to processes of change.

Much has been written already about the dilemmas and difficulties which researchers encounter when working with principles which embrace notions of equity, empowerment and emancipation (Beazley *et al.*, 1997; Barton, 1998; Oliver, 1997; Barnes and Mercer, 1997). This chapter aims to link this debate specifically with issues facing practitioner-researchers within the field of further education.

The research journey on which the chapter is based began in the large College of Further Education in which I work. The context of the research provides an interesting arena for research action, as further education is comparatively under-researched and is also a sector which has undergone enormous change over the last ten years (Mackney, 2003; Harper, 1997). Significant changes began in the early 1990s when FE colleges were 'incorporated' and became free from local education authority control through the Further and Higher Education Act 1992. Local authority control was replaced by more direct governmental control in the guise of a quango, the Further Education Funding Council (superseded by the Learning and Skills Council in 2001). The implications of these changes meant huge growth in student numbers with an agenda of broadening participation situated uncomfortably alongside changeable funding regimes and the loss of many full-time staff across the sector (Mackney, 2003). The research focus of this chapter concerns ways in which disabled students in further education can gain access to financial support – a topic which continues to undergo change within the sector.

The topic of financial support is of great importance to those seeking to widen the inclusion of students in further education as finances can easily constitute a barrier to participation (Holloway, 2001). However, I found conducting research which exposes obstacles disabled students encounter in attempting to maximise funding to participate in further education was problematic. For this reason the chapter has two distinct strands. First there is discussion of how the research topic was chosen and reflection on apparent personal and institutional implications, and second there is an interrogation of the research methods used to conduct an enquiry in the spirit of a participatory action research paradigm.

Since the initial research was undertaken, various modifications have been made to how financial support for students is funded and administered both nationally and within the focal college. However, even the most recent and arguably progressive funding regimes which have since been put in place require ongoing reflection on the extent to which they remove, or conversely shore up, barriers to student participation in further education. This chapter makes a contribution to reflection and the development of further research in the field.

Making initial contact with a research partner

The research was originally designed to meet two broad objectives. It came about as part of an assignment I was undertaking as part of a continuing professional development course. There was a requirement that the project should develop from negotiation with a client group or individual who was to be identified by their apparent marginality in an institutional system. In addition the work was to attempt to bring about positive change in activities which the client group or participating individual had prioritised.

In meeting the first of these two objectives, the following quotation became of significance: 'Enjoy the journey. Getting there isn't important, it's the journey.' This quote comes from Eddie Izzard, comic, actor and now movie star. At the beginning of my research journey I had no idea how important he would be to the focal project, or indeed, how central the concept of enjoyment might be to the research process. However, Izzard and laughter became a significant factor in shaping research relationships and a necessary factor which cemented the possibilities for research action.

I am not sure why I thought about working with Hannah. I had no professional reason to have contact with her but we sometimes shared the lift and she often came close to my office to use an accessible toilet. I noticed Hannah because she was never on her own; she was often with a man I later found out was her partner, or she was with a woman who pushed her wheelchair (described by Hannah as 'my good egg personal assistant'), or she was with a group of children (who I later found out were hers, aged 4, 6, 8 and 10). Often she was with all of them. I really was unsure how I could approach her to discuss the possibility of involving her in research and I took a week to push myself to make the first contact. Notes from the first meeting referred to my great nervousness about approaching her as a possible research participant.

I introduced myself to Hannah one morning while we were both waiting for the lift. I explained I was a lecturer at college but also a student and would like to discuss a research proposal with her if she could spare the time. We agreed to meet in the college Key Skills Centre where she spent a lot of time as it gave her access to study facilities. As my ultimate goal was to carry out research which Hannah would direct I did not want to set out the parameters of my own interests too closely. I began by describing some very vague ideas I had, to do, possibly, with evaluating the college's Disability Statement, as an example of the kind of thing we might research together.

I wanted to make sure Hannah understood that her ideas for a research focus would be equally valid as I hoped we would work together on research which she saw as useful. From the outset I felt it important to be totally honest in explaining to Hannah that I needed her help to work on a project because I was trying to gain a qualification and that involvement would require her to give time. In due course, the issue of time presented real research obstacles for us both, not least because Hannah was studying hard herself as well as managing a home and family. Taking the children to school and picking them up at specific times, for example, meant there could be little flexibility when making arrangements, and particular ways of working were prescribed rather than chosen. The *quid pro quo* was intended to lie in the possibility that what we would spend the time on would be something of real relevance to Hannah. We agreed to meet later that week. I had just finished reading Lois Keith's collection of writings by disabled women, *Mustn't Grumble* (1994), and offered to lend it to Hannah. This gesture turned out to be a strategic enabler of our research relationship because the book helped us to establish important common interests.

Later that week I met Hannah at our agreed time and she was busy using a laptop computer. Her mood was grim, as she was having a great deal of trouble with the size of the keyboard and the small nipple mouse. She told me what a strain it was for her to write and how long everything seemed to take. The idea that our project could involve joint writing seemed untenable. I asked Hannah why she hadn't got her own computer to support her learning at college with an adapted keyboard or voice-activated software. She told me that she had tried to get one but her application had been turned down. And there it was! A real task for a project which would attempt to bring about change which Hannah herself had identified and prioritised: a study of the barriers confronting a disabled student seeking funding through the internal college system.

Evolving a project

We decided we would focus on Hannah's experience of applying for funding as a way of examining the college system for distributing monies. We would research the processes Hannah was actually about to go through: trying to secure funding for a computer. We felt this project would highlight difficulties other students would be likely to encounter and suggest possible avenues for development and change. By attempting to use the college system to apply for real funding, participation in the project had a credible and positive dimension for Hannah; the wider focus on dismantling disabling barriers meant that it was not a project confined to an individual's experience but one which also had wider possibilities for collective development at its core. We decided that on the basis of what we found out we would put forward ideas for development to relevant college staff involved in each stage of Hannah's funding application process and hoped this feedback would benefit other students.

It was agreed that all meetings between us would be confidential. Hannah wanted editorial control over the final written report of the research project and we agreed to work collaboratively as far as we possibly could. Hannah did not wish to have meetings between us tape-recorded. She felt very much as I did, that this would make them stilted, artificial and hamper the free flow of discussion, ideas and thoughts. Instead we followed the practice of Glaser (1998), avoiding tape-recording, and I kept notes of our meetings. I agreed to share any reporting which might be necessary with Hannah before information was disclosed to anyone else.

We reaffirmed our understanding that there was no guarantee that the application for funding would be successful. This was essential, as a fundamental concern at the back of the project was that expectations might be raised which could not be realised. From this time onwards we decided any meetings would be at Hannah's home, as time at college for both of us was very limited. In fact, this seemingly straightforward agreement led us into difficult questions about who had overall control of the research process and became a marker of the extent to which issues of power and control have to be continually negotiated and returned to, despite starting out with a heart-felt commitment to 'working together'.

Funding available to Hannah

At the time of the research, students who faced financial difficulties or whose access to further or higher education might be jeopardised for financial reasons could be supported through Access Funds, introduced by the government in 1990 and provided to FE institutions through the FEFC until 2001. In real terms each student received on average £132 which could be used for fees, books and equipment, transport, child care and accommodation. The national criteria for allocating funds specified that eligible students had to be over 19 and must normally be resident in the United Kingdom for a minimum of three years (i.e. a 'home' student).

A significant report by Kennedy (1997), underscored later by Fryer (1997) and Lane (1998), had recognised funding at both institutional and personal levels as a serious factor in encouraging and maintaining students' participation in further education. At the same time it was being acknowledged that funding was distributed in an apparently random way and policed by the decisions and policies of a range of gatekeepers at national, regional and local levels (Callender and Herbert, 1997). This situation had arisen because each college was allowed to implement mechanisms additional to the national criteria for rationing and targeting their funds. This could be through adding supplementary criteria at the application stage or through its selection and allocation processes.

Working directly with Hannah turned the findings of the previously mentioned reports into graphic reality for me as a researching practitioner. Hannah's life, and the life of her family, had been fundamentally changed by her becoming a student, and the additional costs which this had generated had a significant impact on them all. However, whereas the internal systems which triggered financial support may have seemed equitable, transparent and uncomplicated to staff, they did not always make sense to student applicants. To assist students like Hannah, the college published and made available in a variety of different ways information about the funding procedures in a number of internally produced guides, including *The Student Handbook*, *The College Charter* and *A Student Guide for Money to Study*.

Different realities: our experiences

Hannah made an appointment to see the college Financial Advice Worker and claimed funding to pay for examination fees but was given no advice about any other equipment she could apply for. She said later, 'I was green, I had no idea what I could ask for.' In addition, she found that the process of submitting claims included having to get signatures from tutors and providing four pieces of documentary evidence. This proved a daunting practical task for someone who was not independently mobile.

Working on Hannah's behalf, I began the process of applying for funding for a computer for Hannah to have at home. My experience involved eleven separate activities, including visits to Hannah at home, to staff in college, gathering signatures for approval and checking that all paperwork was completed correctly so that time would not be wasted. I did not have to make appointments to see colleagues from my position as a member of staff and, unlike Hannah, I could easily dash about from one side of the campus to another chasing signatures. I had the luxury of not being reliant on others to provide me with support to aid the process.

Through comparing these experiences, Hannah was able to chart the difficulties she faced both in terms of the general problems related to availability of information and specific obstacles regarding access to staff directly concerned with the Access Fund application. I was also able to experience at first hand the practical difficulties likely to confront many disabled students seeking financial support and observed at first hand the ways in which I was able to minimise them because of my position of relative power within the institution. Table 2.1 shows the difficulties we separately identified.

Hannah worked up a list of actions she felt could improve the experience of other disabled students seeking funding:

- The college should provide a more proactive service so that students know exactly what they are entitled to apply for.
- College to provide a one-stop service so that students with mobility difficulties and part-time students do not need to make lots of additional visits to College.
- Students to be given support in creating an individual data base answering detailed questions related to personal finance that could be kept on file if the student so wished.
- Paperwork, such as copy of enrolment form and timetable, to be provided by college staff.

Table 2.1 Difficulties experienced in relation to the application process

Hannah's experience	My experience
She had no access to a personal tutor, as she was a part-time student	The criteria used to allocate funding were not available for outside examination
Although there was written information in college relating to student financial support, it was muddled with lots of other information	The income and expenditure section of the application form is complex and takes a long time to complete. Many students would give up
Some information seemed contradictory – for example, information related to who could apply for Access Funds stated it was available to students who were unable to start their course because of financial hardship and yet students could only apply once enrolled on a course	The form did not say there was a requirement to provide quotes for specific equipment over a certain cost. This added a number of days to the application process
Key personnel did not seem committed	The people who had 'ownership' of this piece of college procedure were wary about 'outsiders' interfering in their professional space
The building was large, with many levels, and this inevitably led to a lot of physical activity being required when trying to see staff	There was no getting away from having to see lots of people

- All staff involved in the process to have a complete knowledge of what funding and resources are available.
- All staff involved in funding applications to regard such funds as entitlement, not charity, and this to be communicated by their attitude to applicants.

The action list was discussed with the member of staff responsible for the application process and staff involved in its administration and formed the basis of further development and changes in the process.

The key factor Hannah and I had separately exposed as determining a positive or negative experience of making a funding application was the influence individual staff had on the application process at any of its stages. Ongoing staff training seemed to be urgently required. This could be from the simple level of training secretaries to make appointments which fit in with students' time to more complex development such as training to inform the processes of selection of staff on to relevant committees which deal with who should get what and how much.

Some internal changes in funding procedures have subsequently come about through the provision of additional personnel in posts with the purpose of ensuring 'pastoral support' to mature part-time students as well as better methods of informing students about their financial entitlements as part of a Guidance Interview. Information is also now available in various formats such as the Learner Support Guide, which is given out at interview, as well as via the college intranet and Web site. Some things have not changed. There is still a heavy obligation on the individual student to provide documentation required to verify each claim; most of this is necessary for external audit purposes, but the requirement for students to provide more and more documentary evidence complicates, rather than simplifies, the pursuit of funding, particularly for disabled students.

Changes related to the more subtle, interpersonal aspects of the processes involved in seeking funding are more difficult to manipulate and not easily measured. Observations Hannah made about the commitment and attitudes of individual staff were challenging because it was difficult to know how they could be pinned down to specific suggestions for change. Negative observations about my colleagues placed me, as a practitioner-researcher, in an invidious position. I was committed to identifying and removing disabling barriers in my researcher role, whereas my practitioner role bound me in to a code of professionalism which made it difficult to attach those disabling barriers to professional policies or the practices of individual colleagues.

Up to now I have focused mainly on the practical side of the project, which had to do with seeking out funding for the computer and exploring disabling barriers as they arose. As is now becoming clear, another side of the work which needs exploring concerns the many dilemmas, personal struggles and unresolved questions I was personally faced with as a product of the research process. I found out early on that I needed to consider the ethical difficulties of initiating research and making direct contact with disabled people in a much more intimate way than is required, for example, of researchers issuing anonymous questionnaires and working with less direct notions of participation. I constantly examined my meetings with Hannah to interrogate the notion that research can be in some sense 'participative' or 'emancipatory'. The project seemed to be continually transforming my understandings of research practice and of disability issues. I had to keep an open mind on what is meant by 'action research', to continually search for ways of optimising participatory and emancipatory dimensions and try to match my work to various definitions present in the research literature – with which it did not very well accord. Having these confusions at the front of my mind and being prepared to constantly review what I was doing helped me in trying to legitimise the whole activity.

A lingering doubt concerned the idea that what took place was possibly not 'research' at all. A familiar definition of research by Kerlinger used in the work of Cohen and Manion is: 'the systematic, controlled, empirical and critical investigation of hypothetical propositions about the presumed relations among natural phenomena' (Cohen and Manion, 1994, p. 4). But the project with Hannah was not systematic or controlled and no testable hypotheses were put forward. The above-mentioned definition of research did not fit the nature of my enquiry and, as Cohen and Manion later state, the words 'action' and 'research' 'lie as uneasy bedfellows' (Cohen and Manion, 1994, p. 186).

Examining the aims of action research felt a little more comfortable. Elliot's view that *the fundamental aim of action research is to improve practice rather than to produce knowledge* (1991) seemed to lend credence to my way of working. However, Carr observes that the different meanings attached to action research produce confusion:

> Action research now means different things to different people and, as a result, the action research movement often appears to be held together by little more than a common contempt for academic theorising and a general disenchantment with 'mainstream' research. Everybody knows what action research is against. But the important and still unresolved question is: what is it for?
>
> (Carr, 1995, p. 102)

This sense of confusion and uncertainty stayed with me throughout the research process. I was clear that the work undertaken was intended to be about improving practice, and change was indeed seen to come about as a result of both internal and external changes in funding arrangements. Hannah did eventually get a computer as a result of the efforts upon which the research focused. She obtained all the peripherals, aids and assistance needed to help her in her course and I was enriched both personally and professionally by the experience of working with Hannah and meeting her family. However, there is an additional concern: how useful is this research to anyone else? Should research be useful to anyone else?

Vulliamay and Webb discuss these questions and comment that:

> A final perceived limitation of teacher research, and one frequently argued by other educational researchers, is that, whilst such research might lead to improved practice for isolated teachers, the findings are not generalisable to other contexts and cannot be used to advance theoretical understanding.
>
> (Vulliamay and Webb, 1992, p. 18)

However, Vulliamay and Webb also argue that although generalisations may be difficult in this type of work, in-depth studies can be useful in that others can relate such work to their own experiences and through this be offered 'alternative ways of understanding and acting in their own situations' (Vulliamay and Webb, 1992, p. 18).

This brings me back to my first concern – the question of the nature of research and whether the project I was involved with constituted research. I was encouraged by the fact that Ainscow (1998) chose to put the word 'research' in parenthesis when discussing action research and highlighted the important shift involved towards reflection. The idea that research involves one primarily in 'reflection' felt liberating 'without the constrictions associated with traditional research procedures or the predetermined stages of a cycle of the sort recommended in the action research literature' (Ainscow, 1998, p. 16).

I also struggled with determining the extent to which participatory and emancipatory dimensions of research can be integral to action research. Atweh *et al.* put forward a model in which action research encompasses both aspects and much more, saying, 'Action research is a social process. Action research is participatory. Action research is collaborative and practical. Action research is emancipatory. Action research is critical. Action research is recursive' (Atweh *et al.*, 1998, pp. 120–1).

The model is part of a description of research done positioning students as action researchers. It interested me because it was about students as researchers, and Hannah and I were both students, though very differently situated in terms of our student status in the college. The most important aspect of the work described by Atweh *et al.* (1998) is the relative position of the participants in the project which involved students, their teachers and university staff. The writers describe the involvement of students in the research process and talk about their 'selection'. On reading this it seemed incongruous to me that a project that purported to be about a collaborative and potentially emancipatory enquiry into relations between students, teachers and university staff should have an exclusionary process of selection of 'who's in' and 'who's out' of the research built in as part of the research design.

Difficulties to do with the equity of the positions of research participants cannot be ignored or somehow neutralised. In relation to the work with Hannah I was aware that, although I was a student, I was also a college lecturer and in a position of privilege and power, not least of which came from the luxury of studying while earning. In addition, Hannah is a disabled person and I am not. Such multiple positions influence the way that circumstances and events are reported and there is always a strong possibility, as Usher *et al.* point out, that 'in the name of emancipation, researchers (explicitly or implicitly) impose their own meanings on situations rather than negotiate these meanings with research participants' (Usher *et al.*, 1997, p. 196). This was a constant concern for me which I could neither ignore nor fully resolve.

The complexity of our research relations inevitably complicated the nature of the research. Oliver uses a helpful metaphor to clarify the difference between participatory and emancipatory research:

> it seems to me that the former approaches are concerned to allow previously excluded groups to be included in the game as it is whereas emancipatory strategies are concerned about both conceptualising and creating a different game, where no one is excluded in the first place.
> (Oliver, 1996, p. 38)

I had asked Hannah to join my game. My position as a member of college staff gave me the role of team captain. I was financially better resourced than Hannah and had no first-hand experience of disabling barriers. Indeed, Oliver refutes that emancipatory research can actually exist, rather that research should be used as part of an emancipatory process: 'one cannot "do" emancipatory research (nor write methodology cookbooks on how to do it), one can only engage as a researcher with those seeking to emancipate themselves' (Oliver, 1997, p. 25).

From the outset I had hoped to hold on to some principles of participation and emancipation within the project. In reality, Hannah's inclusion in the project was directed by me rather than her; like Atweh, I had 'selected' my research subject. More important, whilst her 'marginality within an institutional system' was noticeable I had no right to assume that she was desirous of 'emancipation'. Towards the end of the project, a member of staff who had given Hannah remarkably little information or support mentioned the possibility of getting a new laptop computer. Hannah replied that she was 'into bigger and better things now', adding, 'I was so controlled. I was so proud of myself.' Perhaps, as Oliver says, it is possible to get evidence of emancipation only after the event. There was evidence that Hannah had grown in confidence as a result of the project work, which had helped her to tackle disabling barriers, but whether she would agree this was 'evidence of emancipation' or linked with the research in any way is hard to gauge.

Looking back

When I began the project I set out with very clear objectives and methods, which I was intending to follow. I was always armed with pen, paper, lists of things to do and specific questions to ask which seemed to give authenticity to my role. As my relationship with Hannah developed, I found it increasingly difficult to maintain this 'professional' stance. The fact that we met most often in the familiar surroundings of her home blurred personal and professional boundaries. Away from college, we found it easy to talk about lots of things and I found I made 'slips' when I shared the criticism of colleagues and the institution voiced by Hannah (see Smith, 1996).

The project was embedded in the belief that many students are marginalised within society and that there is further marginalisation of disabled students. Added to this is the assumption of oppression caused by financial inequalities. In conversation with Hannah and her partner, it was clear that poverty was a more disabling barrier than impairment. At the start of the project I had some reservations about what I was about to do; worries that have been confirmed by other writers. For example Ruth asks, 'Does the laudable intention of giving a voice to the voiceless legitimate the intrusions one might make into the world of the other?' (Ruth, 1997, p. 10).

The longer the project went on, the greater my concern became and the more apologetic I felt I needed to be to Hannah, and increasingly to her partner, for the time I was taking up and for my intrusion into their personal space. Although we had made agreements at the start about what this commitment might mean, we had no real idea of how long the process might take or what other directions we would want to follow. The path we had chosen to follow was certainly not smooth or linear. As Barton had described, it was 'disturbing, complicated, contradictory and extremely demanding in time, thought and emotion' (Barton, 1998, p. 31).

At the end of the project I wanted to spend time with Hannah to discuss some of the issues that had emerged from the research process. I wanted to know how she had felt about the approach I had made in the first place, whether she shared my worries about raising expectations and what barriers existed to being a true co-researcher and the way this could have been managed more effectively.

During this discussion I finally felt I had the confidence to be honest about my feelings. This is not to say that I had ever been dishonest in any of my work with Hannah, but at this culminating point I almost felt honesty was a form of release from the tensions I had felt throughout the project.

Sparkes (1994) in describing the three-year relationship developed from research with one 'subject' comments on the possibility of the process giving the opportunity to 'gain insights into their own self-development by listening to the stories of others. That is, the interaction can serve a therapeutic function for the researcher as well as the subject' (Sparkes, 1994, p. 172).

In much the same way, the project with Hannah had served a range of purposes and was multi-faceted, stretching far beyond what had been originally conceived in terms of coverage.

I confessed the huge sense of responsibility I had felt in relation to the question of raising unrealistic expectations through the enquiry. Hannah had no concerns about the project raising expectations. She said her dealings with other professionals had taught her no one can give absolute guarantees that certain things would take place. We joked that even when she had a cheque in her possession to get her computer, she did not tell anyone else until the boxes of equipment had been delivered to her house. She was open and honest in her replies to questions on her experience of taking part.

She said that how different people would react to the approach we had taken to the project would vary depending on the type of person they were. She described herself as 'a trusting person' and therefore had none of the nervousness that I felt about working together. She did, however, say her partner had voiced some reservations and in retrospect we both should have considered and discussed more fully the impact of what we were undertaking with him. It is worth bearing in mind that research spills into the lives of others who may be only tangentially related to the central project and the opinions and thoughts of significant people closely connected with core research participants should be seriously considered by others embarking on research of this type.

We agreed our biggest difficulty was time and the way that our own personal commitments, both seen and unforeseen, had limited what we were able to do. This was the main reason why Hannah's role of co-researcher had not been developed further. It was a very practical reason, but one which illustrates Oliver's view that true emancipation would have been evidenced only if both of us had initiated the research together at the start as equals.

So what had Hannah got out of the project, if anything, apart from the computer? The word 'therapy' was used by Hannah, the therapeutic effect that comes from having time to talk, to be listened to and to laugh. We had lots of occasions to laugh during our meetings together. She made me laugh about the college's fire evacuation procedures when told from the perspective of someone who would be left in the building to 'wait to be rescued'. She made me laugh in the way she talked disparagingly about 'the walkers' in college, people like me. We both laughed at the humour of Eddie Izzard. Our shared humour led us to keep in touch even after the project had finished.

Confronting professional dilemmas

Some time after the project had been completed it was necessary for me to discuss relevant outcomes with the key personnel involved in the administration of the Learner Support Fund. This was part of my journey to examine the potential of the project as a means to initiate change. I had moved into a different job role and now certain individuals, previously encountered only rarely, were close colleagues whom I met regularly professionally and occasionally socially. I felt great discomfort because they clearly felt criticised by my construction of Hannah's experience and felt it unfairly called to account actions of some staff who no longer worked at the college. There was also a feeling that many of the difficulties Hannah faced had arisen because of externally imposed requirements and restrictions stemming from rules regulating funding that were beyond their control. In fact, the rules on allocation of financial support to disabled students look set to become increasingly stringent in future (LSC 2002). I felt tension when discussing these issues with people I knew worked with great integrity in difficult circumstances. What I appeared to be confronting them with was the criticisms of one individual, Hannah.

The disquiet I felt about this was not anticipated at the start of the project. It was a difficult situation because in some ways discussing the research had turned the focus of the gaze on to Hannah – who could now be perceived as a critical student. I needed to constantly shift the focus back on to disabling barriers, and the tensions between social and individual models of disability were highly visible in these discussions. It is important for others who wish to be engaged in action research within their own workplace to try to anticipate professional dilemmas which will emerge. It now strikes me that finding a way of including the funding gatekeepers in the research process, so that they too could explore the situation alongside Hannah, would have helped to avoid some of the barriers which dissemination of the work started to generate, and change might have been more easily brought about as a result.

Final reflections

Researching the experience of a real person like Hannah can be a powerful method of exposing difficulties that arise because of disabling barriers. On the other hand, focusing on one person's experience may narrow the gaze and induce an 'individual blaming focus' unless the person's experience is constantly interpreted and discussed according to the social model of disability and with due reference to socially created blocks such as discriminatory institutional procedures. Processes can be changed if those in positions of power can be confronted with research evidence that prompts new ways of seeing the causes of disability. The research reported here suggests training based on the social model of disability is imperative in the FE sector to genuinely enhance the participation of disabled students. How disabled people can develop an input into these processes is an important question which, as I hope this chapter has shown, could be further opened up through collaborative research action.

References

Ainscow, M. (1998) 'Would it work in theory? Arguments for practitioner research and theorising in the special needs field', in C. Clark, A. Dyson and A. Millward (ed.) *Theorising Special Education*, London: Routledge.

Atweh, B., Dorman, C. and Dornan, L. (1998) 'Students as action researchers', in B. Atweh, S. Kemmis and P. Weeks (eds) *Action Research in Practice: Partnerships for Social Justice in Education,* London: Routledge.

Barnes, C. and Mercer, G. (1997) 'Breaking the mould? An introduction to doing disability research', in C. Barnes and G. Mercer (eds) *Doing Disability Research,* Leeds: Disability Press.

Barton, L. (1998) 'Developing an emancipatory research agenda: possibilities and dilemmas', in P. Clough and L. Barton (eds) *Articulating with Difficulty: Research Voices in Inclusive Education,* London: Paul Chapman.

Beazley, S., Moore, M. and Benzie, D. (1997) 'Involving disabled people in research', in C. Barnes and G. Mercer (eds) *Doing Disability Research,* Leeds: Disability Press.

Callender, C. and Herbert, A. (1997) *The Funding Lottery: Student Financial Support in Further Education and its Impact on Participation*, London: PSI.

Callender, C. and Smith, N. (1999) *Accessing Funding in FE*, London: FEFC.

Carr, W. (1995) *For Education: Towards Critical Educational Enquiry*, Oxford: Oxford University Press.

Cohen, L. and Manion, L. (1994) *Research Methods in Education,* London: Routledge.

Elliot, J. (1991) *Action Research for Educational Change*, Oxford: Oxford University Press.

Fryer, R. H. (1997) *Learning for the Twenty-first Century*, London: DfEE.

Glaser, Barney G. (1998) *Doing Grounded Theory: Issues and Discussions*, Mill Valley CA: Sociology Press.

Harper, H. (1997) *Management in Further Education: Theory and Practice*, London: David Fulton.

Holloway, S. (2001) 'The experience of higher education from the perspective of disabled students', *Disability and Society* 16 (4), 597–615.

Keith, L. (ed.) (1994) *Mustn't Grumble*, London: Women's Press.

Kennedy, H. (1997) *Learning Works: Widening Participation in Further Education*, London: FEFC.

Kerlinger, F. N. (1996) *Foundations of Behavioural Research*, London: Holt Rinehart & Winston.

Lane Report (1998) *New Arrangements for Effective Student Support in FE*, London: DfEE.

LSC (2002) *FE Learner Support Funds*, LSC.

Mackney, P. (2003) 'Time to rebuild further education', *Lecturer*, May.

Oliver, M. (1996) 'A sociology of disability or a disabilist sociology?' in L. Barton (ed.) *Disability and Society: Emerging Issues and Insights,* London: Longman.

Oliver, M. (1997) 'Emancipatory research: realistic goal or impossible dream?' in C. Barnes and G. Mercer (eds) *Doing Disability Research*, Leeds: Disability Press.

Ruth, D. (1997) 'Facts, power, lies and research', *Educational Action Research* 5 (11), 9–16.

Smith, B. (1996) 'Addressing the delusion of relevance: struggles in connecting educational research and social justice', *Educational Action Research* 4 (1), 73–90.

Sparkes, A. C. (1994) 'Life histories and the issue of voice: reflections on an emerging relationship', *Qualitative Studies in Education* 7 (2), 165–83.

Usher, Bryant, I. and Johnston, R. (1997) *Adult Education and the Postmodern Challenge: Learning beyond the Limits*, London: Routledge.

Vulliamy, G. and Webb, R. (1992) 'The influence of teacher research: process or product?' *Educational Review* 44 (1), 41–58.

Chapter 3

From confusion to collaboration

Can special schools contribute to developing inclusive practices in mainstream schools?

Pauline Zelaieta

As a teacher working from within a special school, how can I work more closely with mainstream colleagues to develop inclusive practices? The very question itself is problematic, even paradoxical – and is packed with educational, political and personal tensions and dilemmas. What is inclusion? How can segregated special schools promote an inclusive educational system? Do my professional practices of working from within a special school contradict my professional and personal commitment to the ideals and values of inclusion?

In this chapter I shall draw on a small action research project to explore some ideas which are sometimes ignored in debates on inclusion and its possible meanings and interpretations. There is a multitude of different, and often contradictory, notions of what constitutes 'inclusion', resulting in confusion and uncertainty about how to interpret inclusive values in terms of our everyday practice. It might seem that this is particularly the case in the context of special schools which, by their very nature, are 'excluding' in that they are separate from the ordinary education settings which most children and young people attend. On the other hand, the education system itself has become increasingly selective and hierarchical and the effects of this are felt within and between schools, and – more broadly – within communities. My starting point, then, is that processes of exclusion and inclusion take place in many ways and at many levels, and that struggles over values and opportunities based on principles of equal participation occur in all kinds of educational settings, including special schools. It is from this perspective that I have begun to explore some of the issues which arose out of my research.

The Alliance for Inclusive Education and Disability Equality in Education views the continuation of segregated special schools as contravening human rights and states that 'Real inclusion cannot happen in a special school' (Mason *et al.*, 2003), highlighting a 'fundamental misconception' of what inclusion is. In complete contrast to this view the New Labour government sees special schools at 'the forefront of the wider education agenda' (DfES, 2003) and emphasises the need to recognise and value their 'unique contribution' within an 'overarching framework of inclusion'.

Dilemmas regarding the continuation of a dual system of special and mainstream educational provision, or 'systematic dualism' (Swain *et al.*, 2003), will continue to be hotly debated for the foreseeable future. In my view, there is an urgent need to minimise the gap between these competing beliefs and views so that inclusion becomes a shared concept and the cultures, policies and practices of mainstream schools can be transformed so that they respond to the interests and social and learning requirements of *all* learners.

Background to the research project

For the past eleven years I have been a teacher in charge of an Inclusion Team, working from within 'Southdown School', which is designated as a school for children identified as having severe, complex and profound learning difficulties, aged between 2 and 11 years. During this time, enthusiastic involvement with a collaborative and supportive role for special schools and a strong commitment to inclusion and increasing learning opportunities through a continuum of provision have been at the core of my working practices. I am a founder member of a group called the Inclusion Forum which is based in 'Elmstown' and consists of professionals from all sectors of the education service in the city. We are concerned with promoting inclusive education for all children, including those who experience difficulties in learning in mainstream settings and we provide a network of support for the practitioners involved.

I began my research as part of a DfES Best Practice Research Scholarship project and it also relates closely to a piece of practitioner research which I carried out as part of a Master's degree in Inclusive Education.

The research

I was concerned with my own role and practice as a leader of an inclusion team and was exploring, questioning and reflecting upon certain areas of my rapidly changing professional world. I wanted to improve the links we had established with mainstream schools and to change their '*ad hoc*' nature, which resulted in patchy and often haphazard approaches to developing inclusive practices. I needed to identify what it is that makes special education 'special' and question the extent of 'expertise' that exists within special schools, disentangling the practices, values and cultures that characterise their work. Once I could begin to understand the contentious nature of 'special' within education, I felt I would be better equipped to begin to explore the procedures and practices which may have a significant impact on students' experience of learning in terms of creating, or removing, barriers to learning and participation, and promote greater inclusion. I needed to begin to examine these tensions and dilemmas prior to any enquiry to establish my own position within the inclusion process. This involved asking the following questions:

- What is inclusion?
- What is *special* about 'special pedagogy'?
- How can a role for special schools be justified in an inclusive educational system?

Although government rhetoric promotes inclusive education, successfully developing these values in day-to-day practice presents difficulties, anxieties and concerns for the very teachers who are keen to promote inclusion in their classrooms. The following concerns voiced by some of these mainstream practitioners involved in my enquiry also helped clarify the initial focus for my research:

- Anxiety with regard to their lack of 'expert' knowledge of issues relating to 'special educational needs' (SEN) in general and in relating these to the inclusion process.
- Difficulty in providing a curriculum that was developmentally appropriate for a wide range of learners.
- Concerns over the formality of lessons and that Literacy and Numeracy Hours actually acted as barriers to inclusion.
- Confusion around the role of support assistants and teachers working together to promote independence and to include individuals within the class as a whole.

The aims

The original aim of my research was to evaluate a partnership between a special school and neighbouring mainstream colleagues within the wider national and local authority context. Through this evaluation I hoped to critically explore ways in which special schools can change their role and work more closely with their mainstream colleagues, supporting the development of educational practices that respond to diversity and encourage the learning and participation of all learners. The prominence given to this 'new role' for special schools by the government, whereby all special schools 'must be outward-looking centres of excellence working with their mainstream partners and other special schools to support the development of inclusion' (DfES, 2001) led me to question my own practices. I needed to understand what I was doing through reflection and exploration and to celebrate, reinforce and, I hoped, improve some aspects of my own working practices.

Initial questions

Initial reflection led me to question how I could significantly engage with change to make an appreciable difference in my own working environment and this eventually led to the formulation of specific questions and methods of enquiry. My primary focus was to enhance inclusive practices in relation to teaching and learning in the mainstream classroom for *all* children, including those identified as having severe and complex learning difficulties. I hoped that this enquiry would help to change the unstructured nature of links we had established with mainstream schools and formalise the process in order to improve our inclusive practices. The initial questions raised at the conceptualisation of this research were:

- What is the extent of the supposed 'expertise' that exists within our school and to what extent could this expertise contribute to developing inclusive education?
- What are the procedures, practices, methods, values and cultures that characterise our work?
- How can we effectively exchange views between ourselves and colleagues in mainstream so that it is mutually supportive and to the benefit of all pupils?

Method

This study has involved taking an action research approach to bring about changes in my working practices. This involved following a cycle of planning, action and critical reflection, which then led to similar cycles of revised planning, action and so on. During this emergent process, the later cycles were shaping my understanding and interpretation of the developments made during the earlier cycles as I was continually refining my methods, data and interpretation through reflection. The research design of this project adopted a multi-method approach, deploying a combination of interconnected empirical approaches, such as personal experience, observations and interviews, in an attempt to develop a deeper understanding of inclusive practices and processes through an interpretative and naturalistic approach. Consultation and collaboration took place with staff from Southdown School, teachers from partnership schools, members of the Inclusion Forum and senior members of staff from other special schools within Elmstown.

Specialist 'expertise'

To enable me to gather evidence relating to the extent of the specialist skills and knowledge, commonly referred to as 'expertise', that exist in our special school, I carried out semi-structured interviews with the teachers working there. The questions concerned teachers' length of service in both mainstream and special schools, their initial specialist teacher training and any additional specific qualifications they might have. The main purpose of this initial survey was to try and establish whether teachers really did possess any clearly discernible 'expertise' and if they did, to identify the extent to which teachers in our school had gained their 'expertise' through formal qualifications and training rather than through straightforward experience.

Defining 'special pedagogy'

Before I could examine how special schools can diversify and share specialist skills and knowledge with mainstream colleagues, there was a need to define 'specialist skills and knowledge' in the context of Southdown School. I carried out a group interview with fifteen teachers at Southdown School and time was set aside during a weekly staff meeting for this to take place. I then asked fifteen mainstream teachers what specialist skills and knowledge they thought existed in a special school and how they could best share this 'expertise' with them.

In order to approach the question of assumed expertise from a number of vantage points, I decided to observe ten Literacy Hour sessions, five in mainstream schools where a child identified as having complex needs was present, and five in Southdown School. These were non-participant observations, using a detailed observation checklist in which all the main features and activities in the classroom were observed, such as the physical features of the room, materials used and teacher and pupil interactions within the classroom.

Link schemes

In an attempt to glean an overall picture of the present position of link schemes between special and mainstream schools that are under way in Elmstown, I gathered information from two sources. One source was a focus group, which was arranged to discuss local link schemes, and the other source was a Special School Conference, which focused on sharing current inclusive practices in Elmstown. The focus group consisted of eight members of the Inclusion Forum, including professionals from mainstream schools, special schools and support services from within Elmstown. The discussion focused on present inclusive practices, barriers that were perceived to hinder further progression and possible ways forward to improve present inclusive practices.

The Special School Conference consisted of members of senior staff representing eleven of the fourteen specialist schools in Elmstown and various LEA advisory staff and the aims of the conference were:

- To share and document current educational and social inclusion and reintegration practice.
- To agree the principles of an inclusion policy for special schools.

During the day, each specialist school in Elmstown gave a short presentation describing its practices relating to inclusion and identified certain difficulties that they had to overcome.

Contrasting visions of inclusion

Prior to evaluating the findings of the research in respect of improving and formalising mainstream links with Southdown School, it is important to discuss how the research has affected my critical thinking with regard to the initial dilemmas that were discussed earlier in this chapter.

Definition of inclusion

During the research process, it emerged that most of the participants agreed that inclusion relates to the principles and processes that are involved in increasing a school's capacity to respond to pupil diversity and promote greater participation for all pupils. It is concerned with developing broad learning strategies to foster inclusion as an alternative to individual provision based on perceptions of individual 'special needs', and is seen as an ongoing process which focuses on school organisation and culture. Inclusion relates to a commitment and responsibility to the process of restructuring schools so that they respond to the diversity of pupils in their locality (Booth and Ainscow, 1998; Booth et al., 2000; Swain et al., 2003).

Integration on the other hand is viewed as a mechanism in which individual pupils are expected to adapt to conditions and practices in ordinary schools (Armstrong et al., 2000). It is a device concerned with fitting children into existing systems and focuses on *where* pupils are educated rather than *how*.

During the study, as organisations defined their 'vision' of inclusion, conflicting interpretations and priorities began to emerge. For example, the focus of the inclusion team at Southdown School was on transferring specialist skills and knowledge to enable mainstream schools to include all children in their community. Another special school stated that their principal concern was to include their pupils in their families and that teaching them to live in society post-16, focusing on social and emotional skills, was central to their inclusive philosophy. Yet another special school maintained that inclusion for special schools was not about transporting students around the city, but about maximising the learning potential of all the staff and children in the special school itself. In stark contrast, the 'vision' of inclusion of the local authority was framed in terms of reducing the number of exclusions in the city (as a result of schools' policies on behaviour or non-attendance on the part of pupils) and to increase overall attendance levels.

One could question whether one vision of inclusion was more 'inclusive' than another. For example, is a focus on *educational* inclusion more inclusive than a focus on *social* inclusion? Is an 'inward-looking' focus on the cultures, practices and policies of a special school more or less 'inclusive' than an 'outward-looking' focus on developing mutually supportive links and partnerships with mainstream colleagues? In conclusion, it was accepted that these different interpretations raised key issues for which there are no fixed or formulaic right or wrong answers; they simply reflect the different perspectives and priorities of each organisation or community, and how these are interpretated in terms of a 'vision of inclusion'. This is not to argue that one interpretation of inclusion is as good as another, but simply to point out that principles relating to rights and values are complex, and how they are understood will vary between contexts. It is important, therefore, to try to understand and learn from these different points of view and this involves *listening* and working collaboratively.

Special pedagogy

Although teachers interviewed during this study agreed that inclusion was generally about children's rights, it was the effectiveness of the education that the children received in the classroom that was their main concern. Rose (2002) and Lindsay (2003) also make clear distinctions between a focus on ethics and rights and a focus on efficacy. They maintain that in order to influence the effectiveness of the education that children receive, we need to move forward from a single focus on the rights and needs of disabled people to also include a focus on the practicality of how we can include all children effectively.

Through detailed classroom observations and interviews with teachers, it was recognised that in order to provide effective education and respond to pupil diversity, there would sometimes be a need to implement particular teaching approaches with specific children at various times. It was also argued that many children experiencing difficulties in learning were seen to need some distinct kinds of teaching at certain times, alongside common teaching approaches at other times. These observations concur with Lewis and Norwich (2001), who suggest that this 'continuum' of teaching approaches enables us to distinguish between the 'normal' adaptations in class teaching for the majority of pupils and the more specialist adaptations required for those who experience more severe difficulties in learning. In conclusion, in order to provide *all* children with effective educational experiences, 'special pedagogy' should be viewed as an integral part of the inclusion process, as some 'specialist adaptations' will be needed for some children for some of the time. It is not clear, however, whether the use of the term 'special' in relation to teaching and learning is useful, in that many approaches adopted in special schools may well be useful in developing inclusive practices in mainstream schools, involving all learners.

Is there a role for special schools within the inclusion process?

The continued existence of special schools is viewed by many as a major barrier to inclusive education in which all children will be welcomed in community schools on an equal basis, regardless of difference. Historically, special schools and mainstream schools have been placed at conflicting and opposing ends of a continuum. Positioned at one extremity are the 'experts' with their specialist skills and knowledge whose training is seen as 'highly advanced, extensive and intensive' (Dyson, 2001) and as institutions that have a 'vast wealth of knowledge, skills and experience which, if harnessed, unlocked and effectively utilised by mainstream schools, can help ensure that inclusion is a success' (DfES, 2003). This is counterbalanced by the opposing position of those who view segregated schooling as violating children's right to inclusion and those who challenge the legitimacy of special education and its contribution to 'the manufacture and maintenance of segregation' (Thomas and Loxley, 2001).

If views that are critical of special education are justified, how can special schools and special educators in particular be instrumental in developing inclusive practices? As identified at an early stage of this research, despite a commitment to inclusion, many mainstream teachers are experiencing anxieties, difficulties and concerns in embedding inclusive values in their day-to-day practices. The challenge to educate pupils identified as having complex difficulties in learning may be seen as insurmountable to teachers who have no experience of responding to these great challenges, but, as MacKay (2002) contests, 'theirs is not a hard reaction to overcome if they are willing to learn from the experience of others'. My research suggested that special schools in the city are closely linked with the inclusion process and could be viewed as 'a valuable source of intellectual capital' (Attfield and Williams, 2003), sharing experiences of changing curriculum, organisation and attitudes, helping mainstream staff to gain the 'confidence and skills to tackle issues arising in the successful inclusion of individual pupils' (Attfield and Williams, 2003).

Far from being a barrier to inclusive education, the research found that the special schools involved welcomed inclusion and were often the instigators of initiatives to promote inclusion, and their commitment to overcoming exclusionary barriers is illustrated in the following examples.

The Inclusion Forum

The Inclusion Forum was originally founded by eight special school teachers who were struggling to promote inclusive practices in the context of their own work contexts. Much was gained from the opportunities presented for mutual support, networking and dissemination of current practice. Regular discussions ranging from general philosophical debates around inclusive education to practical solutions to specific issues were important features of our earlier meetings. This proactive forum now has over 100 members on its mailing list and has joined forces with two other significant inclusion groups in Elmstown, providing a potentially powerful link between the local education authority, professionals and parents at grass-roots level. The goals of the forum include:

- To share the experiences and good practice of including children who experience difficulties in learning in mainstream settings and to provide a network of support for the practitioners involved.
- To liaise with the local education authority, other agencies and professionals to improve opportunities for pupils to be included in their local mainstream school.
- To develop a coherent strategy for inclusive education across the age ranges – from nursery to further education.

Although the forum has seen many changes over the years and involves professionals from all sectors of the education service, special school teachers remain the driving force at the hub of the organisation. Those involved have positively welcomed inclusion and played a key role in instigating the development of inclusive initiatives in Elmstown. Representatives from the Inclusion Forum were involved in a task force set up by the local education authority concerned with advising on the formation of a strategic plan for special education needs in the city. This provided a number of opportunities for debating issues relating to exclusion and inclusion.

Fluidity between special and mainstream

During my research I found evidence of a commitment to inclusive education on the part of some special schools in the way that they were 'desegregating' some of their pupils through their gradual transfer into mainstream settings. For example, one child from Southdown School increased her time in mainstream from one to two sessions a week, which was then increased to being dually placed, meaning she attended her local mainstream school for three days a week and Southdown School for two days a week. This reached a successful conclusion whereby she was soon attending her local mainstream school full-time. Another child was dually placed with his local mainstream school and Southdown, and this also resulted in his full-time attendance at the mainstream school.

Through experience, we have found that this gradual approach to transition, coupled with continual support for the mainstream school, not only helps pupils to adjust to the mainstream setting, but also helps to break down fears and anxieties experienced by the mainstream staff, both of which are essential components to the success of such placements. When support for mainstream schools is not forthcoming, there is a danger, particularly for pupils who experience complex difficulties in learning, of 'inappropriate mainstreaming' (MacKay, 2002), which does not meet the social or educational needs of the individual or those of their classmates. For example, one pupil attending mainstream school full-time was finding the day-to-day pressures of school life extremely difficult and was telling us this through his behaviour. The teachers at the school were also facing very difficult challenges in including him within the structured daily class and school routines. Transferring him part-time to a special school helped to ease the immediate pressure on the pupil as well as the school. This resulted in the pupil regaining much of his confidence and gave the staff the opportunity of much needed support from the special school. At present, the pupil may spend less time in his mainstream school, but if this school develops in terms of transforming its culture and practices so that differences are celebrated and all pupils are welcomed and provided for on a basis of equality, the situation will change. The arrangement remains flexible and the balance of time spent at each school is kept under constant review, especially by means of 'listening' to the perspective of the pupil. This example highlights the real and urgent need for mainstream schools to change, so that pupils such as the one just referred to are not excluded from their local school and are not required to attend *two* different schools, unlike the rest of the population.

These examples suggest that special education can play a key role in the inclusion process and is, at present, an essential component of the evolving continuum of inclusive provision. Special schools need to concentrate on practical ways in which they contribute to moving the inclusion process forward, rather than taking up a defensive position. Although at present there is a role for some special schools, it will ultimately change and disappear completely as mainstream schools transform themselves into communities for all learners.

Evaluating the findings

The need for support and professional development for mainstream schools to further their inclusive practices has been recognised for a number of years. My research suggests that there must also be opportunities for staff from both schools to work collaboratively, including shared professional development opportunities for curriculum planning and teaching. There should also be opportunities for teachers and support staff to teach and support both mainstream children and children who have additional learning needs, which, in turn, will help to overturn the predisposition to focus solely on the assumed 'expertise' of special educationalists. As this research identified, both special and mainstream teachers have aspects of 'expertise' with regard to recognising in their practice the commonality and uniqueness of all learners, which, if used in collaboration, would increase the quality and flexibility of teaching approaches and further extend participation in learning on democratic principles.

Link schemes

Although the role of link schemes in aiding the inclusion process has often met with scepticism, this study suggests that the setting up of link schemes can play an important role in the development of inclusion. I found that, in general, the mainstream education system is not yet ready or, possibly, even prepared to adjust its practices sufficiently to meet the needs of those who experience the most complex and challenging difficulties. Pupils may be physically present in classrooms, but they will be *included* only if they are able to participate and take an active part in group and class activities. One teacher told us:

> With no previous experience of teaching children with profound and multiple learning difficulties, I found including Jane in class activities extremely difficult. Southdown Inclusion Team helped me to identify appropriate learning objectives for Jane, which enabled me to respond to her individual needs and learning styles, which in turn ensured that she could access and be included in group activities.
>
> (Teacher 1)

While this kind of collaboration is crucial, it does not in itself ensure that cultural change is taking place in terms of the ethos and practices of the school. Without transformational change at all levels, Jane will not be a full, equal member of the school community. However, the kind of collaborative working described above, and the overcoming of perceived barriers and difficulties on the level of teaching and learning, can play a key role in changing minds and practices.

Barriers to link schemes

Although most special schools contributing to the research project reported positively on the development of their various inclusive practices, a very large proportion reported that they wished to do more but were restricted by financial constraints. One school reported, 'We are frustrated at not being able to develop this work further and it leaves us feeling undervalued. Inclusion work is one of the most beneficial things we do' (Teacher 2). Another school stated that:

> Inclusion cannot be done on the cheap. Inclusive initiatives need a proper activity-led funding formula which applies to all special schools

otherwise we will not move forward from the present array of ad-hoc initiatives which are carried out on a shoestring.

(Teacher 3)

In rank order, the principal factors perceived by teachers to inhibit the formation of link initiatives in Elmstown were:

- Financial constraints.
- Lack of leadership.
- Problems with the local education authority.
- Organisational difficulties.
- The prevalence of 'ad hoc' initiatives.
- Resistance from mainstream.
- Negative attitudes of staff.
- Staffing difficulties.
- Transport problems.
- Pressure on mainstream schools.
- Lack of time.

At the time of the research there was a lack of a shared vision for inclusion in the local education authority and confusion ensued as to what this meant in practical terms for special schools. One teacher in the Inclusion Forum commented that:

Because there is no substantial LEA guidance for special schools, it's been left to individual schools to set their own priorities for change. This means any initiatives have been patchy and fragmented rather than schools being able to maximise their success through a clear and cohesive framework. I would say that this, in my opinion, is one of the biggest barriers to progression.

(Teacher 4)

This lack of clarity was a key factor in the development of 'ad hoc' initiatives' and further highlights the importance of establishing a shared understanding of 'inclusion'. Until a shared vision of inclusion and a framework for change is established in Elmstown, special schools will carry on 'tinkering at the edges', unable to fully prioritise the day-to-day issues involved in the inclusion process and maximise their success.

Questions raised

If future link schemes are to be successful, they should focus on the significant questions that this study has raised. For example:

- Is there a common understanding of the concept of inclusion?
- What kind of forum is needed so that questions and differences can be openly discussed?
- Is there a workable balance between 'common' and 'specialist' pedagogy?
- Have both mainstream teachers and teachers in special schools developed the knowledge, understanding and skills required to work effectively with all children, including those identified as having severe or complex learning difficulties?
- Do all teachers understand the advantages of mutual collaboration?
- Are priorities for change set within a clear and cohesive framework?

Specialist skills and knowledge

My study identified areas of specialist skills and knowledge perceived to be present by teachers at Southdown School and compared them with the perceptions of mainstream teachers about the existence of those skills and how we could best share 'expertise' with them. The results were analysed and five areas of potential support are identified in Box 3.1.

Teachers also identified a desire to raise understanding of the creativity of special schools to meet a wide range of needs through experiencing real-life experiences. They felt that access to specialist practices should be an integral part of initial teacher training programmes in order to help develop strategies to teach a wide range of pupils identified as having intellectual, communicative and multiple disabilities in mainstream classrooms. Through this research, I would argue that there are no 'experts' in special education. Put simply, teachers working in segregated settings have had different working experiences from those working in mainstream schools. It is in the mutual sharing of the collective wealth of diverse experiences that the key to providing an equitable educational system which incorporates both the commonality and uniqueness of all learners can be found. This mutual partnership between teachers working in both mainstream and special schools is instrumental in overcoming barriers to participation and learning, and to developing the greater inclusion of all pupils in the cultures, curricula and communities of their schools.

Bringing about change

On the basis of my research experience, I believe that in order to further the inclusion process from purely a discourse of ethics to include one of action, several priorities need to be addressed. The concept of inclusion is not just about the complexity of definition, or simply about rights, values and ideologies. It is clear that there is a need for a shared perception of the practical realisation of inclusion and that until there is a mutual understanding between the government, local education authorities, schools, other

Box 3.1 Five areas of general support

General support

- Confidence-building, general encouragement and support
- Lending resources
- More liaison between mainstream and special
- General awareness building with regard to inclusive practices, working with whole families, teaching and learning styles, etc.
- Involvement in Personal, Social and Health Education (PSHE) lessons so that a more informed view on disability can be put across to pupils

Training in specific teaching methods

- Use of communication aids, symbols, sign language, TEACCH techniques, etc.
- Behaviour plans and strategies

Curriculum adaptation and assessment

- Knowledge of national adapted schemes of work, assessments, e.g. P levels
- Advice on adapting the curriculum and identifying a range of alternatives in curriculum delivery
- Suggesting appropriate activities, etc.
- Help with differentiating lessons and materials
- Help with setting finely graded targets
- Help formulating Individual Education Plans (IEPs), assessments, etc.

Awareness of the needs of the child

- Awareness of physical/sensory needs of children
- Awareness of safety issues
- Independence skills: making choices, problem solving and allowing time to respond
- Seeing the whole child and adapting teaching styles to match individual learning styles

Classroom management

- Practical help with class management: working as a team, including children
- Working in a multi-professional team, including speech and language therapist, physiotherapist, occupational therapist, etc.

professionals, parents, voluntary groups and individuals, any change in the role of special schools is particularly difficult.

A framework for mutual partnership

In order to overcome some of the difficulties already discussed, there is a need to develop a framework for future partnerships which includes the following:

- A shared vision and clearly defined purpose.
- Formality of link established from the outset.
- Involvement of parents and a commitment to listening to the perspectives of pupils.
- Permanent commitment from all schools involved in the partnership.
- Mutual staff respect for knowledge and experience.
- Joint professional development opportunities for staff.
- Collaborative approaches to curriculum planning and teaching.
- Good liaison between all parties involved.
- Commitment to equality of opportunity and treatment.
- Ongoing monitoring, assessment and evaluation of the partnership.

As schools begin to critically engage in the often painful process of self-analysis and reflection, we hope we will begin to see a significant shift away from exclusive discourses and practices and see schools involved in collaborative and mutually supportive work in support of inclusion in education, culminating in the transformation of the very system itself.

Conclusion

My principal concern at the beginning of the research process was to improve the links that had been established between our special school and mainstream schools and to change their unstructured nature which resulted in patchy and haphazard approaches to developing inclusive practices. The challenge was to develop a research strategy that would inform and acknowledge my own position as a practitioner and interpretive researcher, and the key to this goal was to look at how I could engage with change to make a significant difference in my own working environment. The key issues that emerged from this small project have been revealing and informative and have served not only to bring about change within my own practice, but also to begin to build bridges between political rhetoric and actual practice.

This study has made a considerable contribution to my understanding of inclusive issues, particularly with regard to the role of special schools in the inclusion process. It has also contributed to Southdown School's ability to unlock its knowledge, skills and experience in an attempt to ensure that these specialist practices are made useful to mainstream schools to aid the successful inclusion of all pupils. As with any research project, the study unearthed more questions, issues and dilemmas than it answered. The next stage of my research cycle will involve investigating one of these major issues by examining the role of support assistants in the inclusion process. How can we ensure that support assistants reinforce the role of the teacher, facilitate independent learning and help, rather than hinder, the inclusion of individual pupils? Yet again, the very question itself is problematic and packed with educational, philosophical and personal tensions and dilemmas . . .

References

Armstrong, F., Belmont, B. and Verillon, A. (2000) '"Vive la différence"? Exploring context, policy and change in special education in France: developing cross-cultural collaboration', in F. Armstrong, D. Armstrong and L. Barton (eds) *Inclusive Education: Policy, Contexts and Comparative Perspectives*, London: David Fulton.

Attfield, R. and Williams, C. (2003) 'Leadership and inclusion: a special school perspective', *British Journal of Special Education* 30 (1), 28–33.

Booth, T. and Ainscow, M. (eds) (1998) *From Them to Us: an International Study of Inclusion in Education*, London: Routledge.

Booth, T., Ainscow, M., Black-Hawkins, K., Vaughan, M. and Shaw, L. (2000) *Index for Inclusion: Developing Learning and Participation in Schools*, Bristol: Centre for Studies on Inclusive Education.

DfES (2001) *Inclusive Schooling: Children with Special Educational Needs*, Nottingham: DfES Publications.

DfES (2003) *The Report of the Special Schools Working Group*, Nottingham: DfES Publications.

Dyson, A. (2001) 'Special needs in the twenty-first century: where we've been and where we're going', *British Journal of Special Education* 28 (1), 24–9.

Lewis, A. and Norwich, B. (2001) *A critical review of systematic evidence concerning distinctive pedagogies for pupils with difficulties in learning.* Online www.nasen.uk.com/ejournal/000036_000122.php> (accessed 16 April 2003).

Lindsay, G. (2003) 'Inclusive education: a critical perspective', *British Journal of Special Education* 30 (1), 3–15.

MacKay, G. (2002) 'The disappearance of disability? Thoughts on a changing culture', *British Journal of Special Education* 29 (4), 159–63.

Mason, M., Whittaker, J., Shaw, L., Reiser, R. and Simpson, D. (2003) 'Government Breaks Promise on Inclusion for Disabled Children', press release to coincide with the publication of the DfES *Report of the Special Schools Working Group* issued by the Alliance for Inclusive Education, the Bolton Institute, the Centre for Studies on Inclusive Education, Disability Equality in Education and Parents for Inclusion.

Rose, R. (2002) 'A Future Role for Special Schools in Supporting Inclusion', paper presented at Equals Conference, Imperial College, London, July.

Swain, J., French, S. and Cameron, C. (2003) *Controversial Issues in a Disabling Society*, Buckingham: Open University Press.

Thomas, G. and Loxley, A. (2001) *Deconstructing Special Education and Constructing Inclusion*, Buckingham: Open University Press.

Chapter 4

Forging and strengthening alliances

Learning support staff and the challenge of inclusion

Catherine Sorsby

The action research project presented in this chapter emerged from years of personal and professional questioning towards an understanding of the breadth and depth, and the principles and possibilities, which inclusive education provides. For me, action research is about asking questions – questions I need to know the answers to in order to improve my work. It involves wondering why I am doing things in a particular way – particularly if I've been directed to do something I find ineffectual. It doesn't matter to me if the questions aren't relevant to the wider audience of the local education authority or DfES. What matters is that through research action I can find a more effective way of achieving something or enhance my support of others. I have discovered that doing action research develops confidence: empowering not only me as the researcher, but also raising the confidence of others whose voices can be heard during the research process. I have found my own action research often challenging the status quo which can be immensely satisfying and enlightening but also unsettling. Either way, doing research can make a major contribution to personal and professional development. This chapter describes the sort of ordinary research action I get involved in, with ordinary people in an ordinary, average school. It provides an insight into the different learning experiences of the staff who participate in research with me and details some of the many unexpected benefits discovered en route. Hopefully it will encourage staff in other schools to undertake similar projects by demonstrating that simple collaborative enquiry can sow the seeds of change far more effectively than the imposition of new policy and practice by traditional 'cascade' models of training and communication.

Support for support staff

Over the course of my career it has concerned me that teams of workers in mainstream schools, frequently referred to as the 'non-teaching staff' or the 'child care assistants' are routinely under-supported. Some have NNEB nursery nurse qualifications whereas others possess few formal academic qualifications. None the less, these colleagues often have obvious talents in child care, psychology, behaviour management or developing communication skills which they demonstrate daily by getting straight to the heart of any problem and coming up with practical solutions.

I began to realise the training needs of non-teaching staff are commonly neglected when I became an INSET co-ordinator. A lack of professional development seems to have left non-teaching staff feeling in a passive position within the context of their work. In my observation, they are seldom invited to participate in staff meetings or training events, but they can be asked to do cleaning or redecorating during the time set aside for other people's development. They may not be deliberately excluded, but there is often an assumption that it is unfair to expect them to attend meetings or to undertake training. When I have asked individuals why they are not more assertive about their aspirations for their work, replies go along the lines of 'It's not up to me, I just do as I'm told.' In the past I have felt that many non-teaching staff I worked with were resistant to suggestions of training opportunities. As a newly appointed INSET co-ordinator I saw a difficult task ahead of me, particularly when I noticed that the National SEN Specialist Standards called for Learning Support Assistants who:

> appreciate how their roles relate to, and complement, those of the teaching staff; contribute positively to the establishment of school policies and plans, and apply these consistently to secure effective pupil management and achievement of pupils' targets; encourage independence in learning; work co-operatively with teachers, parents/carers and others to realise targets set out in individual education and care plans; make good use of formal and informal opportunities to increase their personal expertise and that of the service or school they represent.
>
> (TTA, 1999, p. 52)

In view of the new expectations around roles it seemed derisory to continue to refer to the group I was thinking about as non-teaching assistants. In this chapter I use the term *Learning Support Assistants* (LSAs) to refer to those adults (other than teachers) employed to work with, and support, children in the classroom situation. Job titles and descriptions vary from one local education authority to another, and even from school to school within the same LEA, but the term LSA seems an appropriate generic term.

As a newcomer to the school it was easy to observe that non-teaching support staff worked conscientiously and fairly effectively. However, it was also easy to observe that they occupied a low position in the school's professional hierarchy and they did not have the benefit of equal opportunities for continuing professional development. My impression was also that support staff seemed to have a unique perspective on the culture of the school and on the balance of power within it. I hoped that carrying out research would prompt some form of change, either by giving the LSAs a voice, or by increasing their opportunities for training, or both.

Beginning action research

As has been said in the opening chapter of this book, one of the early stages of an action research project involves familiarisation with the broader picture, including reading related literature and policy documents. Much of what I had read confirmed perceptions about the lack of guidance, structure and career development opportunities for learning support assistants (e.g. Balshaw, 1991; Bell, 1998; Clayton, 1989a, b, 1990a, b; Fox, 1993; Woolf and Bassett, 1988). More recent publications confirmed that many of these difficulties are ongoing (Farrell *et al.*, 2000; O'Brien and Garner, 2001). Recurrent concerns include lack of opportunities for training, inadequate career structure, no performance management and a disappointing lack of rewards in terms of job satisfaction or remuneration. Non-teaching staff are seldom engaged in consultation and experience directives about their work as imposed in a top-down manner. Their roles and responsibilities are frequently unclear and the voices of support staff are seldom heard (O'Brien and Garner, 2001).

Early investigations in my own school revealed a complex variety of job titles and a range of frequently overlapping job descriptions illogically tied to different levels of remuneration. I could see how contractual ambiguity had developed historically but realised it opened the way for the possible exploitation of support staff, and misuse of their skills and experience. It was evident that teaching staff were unaware of inequity and the support staff themselves did not have full knowledge of the complexity of the situation. A plan for an action research project began to take shape.

First steps

Through observation and the use of a series of questionnaires, semi-structured interviews, and an audit of policies and other school documents, I began to clarify the expectations and the roles and responsibilities of the support staff. I investigated their training needs, both in terms of the way the support staff themselves identified them and from my own perspective. This clarified issues and provided a sense of direction so the challenge of bringing about change began to seem feasible.

The struggle for change was multi-layered and was concerned with issues of democracy and empowerment, and the entitlement of non-teaching staff to the same opportunities for training, access to information and professional development as their teaching peers. Once training opportunities were made available to support staff they began, albeit hesitantly, to take up the opportunities on offer. Some began to recognise missed opportunities and to develop career aspirations. Several drew on the school's INSET budget to pay for LEA training courses and some sought funding from the DfEE Individual Learning Accounts (ILAs). Others welcomed news from the Local Government National Training Organisation (February 2000) that NVQs were being developed for Teaching Assistants as part of the project to produce National Occupational Standards, but then found that they had to wait months for courses to be provided locally. However, as they began to increase their range of skills and qualifications they also began to question and voice opinions. For example, one assistant commented, 'Class teachers could do with a course on how to manage CCA support in classrooms . . . to make more effective and appropriate use of me.' I was pleased to see some of the LSAs becoming more assertive. It seemed research action had initiated real change and over the coming months I developed an interest in capitalising upon this.

Towards inclusion – an impossible leap?

Following on from the DfEE Green Paper (1997) and the proposed programme of action (DfEE, 1998), the LEA published its own SEN strategy which clearly and frequently stated that one of the aims was 'to develop an increasingly inclusive education system', and that 'by 2003 all children with SEN may have their needs met within educational provision in their local community'. There seemed to be an obvious need for information, training and support for planning to be provided for LSAs to facilitate the proposed moves towards inclusive education. It seemed imperative to complement an agenda for inclusion of all pupils with a parallel agenda respecting the right of school staff to experience inclusion in their working lives. Yet policies and practices were being implemented that excluded a significant contingent of LSAs from key development opportunities. I was also troubled by the notion that the development of an inclusive culture was primarily seen as relevant to those children identified as having 'special educational needs' whereas other aspects of identity could be key determinants of exclusion.

I then came across a powerful resource in the form of the *Index for Inclusion* (Booth *et al.*, 2000). In this document it was clearly stated that 'inclusion is for staff as well as pupils' and this encouraged me to seek to explore the perspective of the LSAs on inclusion matters. The material in the *Index for Inclusion,* and the experience of carrying out my own research using the index as a research tool, took on new meaning, as I had recently started to use a wheelchair. I began to experience at first hand what it is like to be excluded from key aspects of school life – which I knew to be the ordinary course of things for LSAs in school.

Opportunities for action research were tantalising, yet the clear aim of attempting to bring about change in the management structures and cultures of the school when I was a single voice and neither a member of the Senior Management Team nor a SENCO narrowed the scope considerably. However, I saw no reason why I should not try to extend the knowledge and skills of myself and the support staff who, in the usual course of events, would probably be the last to be involved in consultation or training.

Second steps

The first step in my small-scale action research project had enabled clarification of the expectations, roles and responsibilities of support staff and prompted an investigation of their training needs. Preliminary research action provided the basis of a general plan that would be the first part of a new action research process. I obtained DfES funding in the form of a Best Practice Research Scholarship and additional funding from the LEA to enable further work with LSAs to explore understanding of the concept of inclusive education and to introduce the *Index for Inclusion* as an audit tool. I hoped further research engagement would determine what support LSAs would need to enable them to further the project of inclusion, enable some insight into how the proposed NVQs and National Standards might benefit our staff and provide scope for evaluation of a range of other induction and/or training packages available from the DfES, LEA and other sources.

Although these were my stated aims, I expected difficulties if I was to encourage the group of LSAs to take some ownership of the research project and to accept some responsibility for the development of agendas for discussion. I had received funding to meet specific aims and realised this placed my work at odds with my stated commitment to empowering the LSAs to determine their priorities for research action. I tried to resolve this by involving them as openly as possible from an early stage, and indeed by sharing the dilemma.

I chose a target group of four adults as representatives of the thirteen support staff employed in the school as they had differing job titles, roles and responsibilities, and length of term of employment in the school. One of them was also a governor at the school. I invited them to a series of morning workshops to be held in school time once a week for eight weeks. The funding paid for supply cover for everyone involved. Our task involved planning, monitoring, evaluating and reflecting on the progress made through the series of workshops. I called the sessions 'workshops' to reflect the concept of equality: I had no intention of taking on the role of trainer to a group of trainees. There were some things they could learn from me, but I needed to learn from them too. By preparing tentative agendas for the first three sessions I was able to encourage participants to voice their opinions and to encourage them to take responsibility for the agendas of the remaining meetings. The LSAs kept my original aims in mind, but enriched the project by broadening the scope of the discussions beyond my earlier ideas.

Data collection methods included observations and recording of comments made by the LSAs. Their comments, recorded in my research diary, reflected changing attitudes over a number of weeks as they were exposed to other perspectives and challenged to justify their own observations and opinions. The group discussions were often lively debates over provocative comments I found through articles, books or Internet sites debating the contentious nature of the issue of inclusion. As one LSA said:

> there was much supportive information to assist our understanding. We were encouraged to be open and truthful in our discussions. I was shocked by some of my feelings, which I have to say changed sometimes from week to week.
>
> (Comments from participant LSA)

At the end of the project my research diary revealed that as a group we had reflected on our own experiences and considered evidence concerning the changing role of LSAs in the school, the changing needs of the children, the changing structure and culture of the school. We had also discussed issues such as roles and responsibilities, the formulation of school policies and practice, planning and preparation times, consultation, collaborative working practices, evaluation of their work in the classroom, career progression, LEA and DfES policies on either the work of support staff or inclusion. Through exploration and questioning of each other, we had discovered alternative ways of supporting children. I had noted that the LSAs had found it enlightening when they were given the opportunity to examine documents they did not usually have access to. We were able to examine and review a number of induction and training packages, and discuss their relative merits and relevance in terms of our respective work contexts and experience.

Viewing videos produced by a local school on aspects of inclusive education, such as links between mainstream and special schools and dual placements, led to some lively debate and a strong desire to visit other schools to observe different examples of interesting practice. I was able to arrange for the LSAs to visit three local primary schools. The learning opportunities afforded by those visits were a highlight of the project, with every member of the project group requesting further opportunities to meet, and observe, LSAs in other schools:

> I hadn't realised that staff could be deployed in such a different way. Their idea of timetabling was so much more flexible than ours. The class teachers were full of praise for the assistants and said they organised themselves well. They were very laid back about the situation and there was such a calm atmosphere in the room. I noticed so many different ways of doing things, I just wanted to talk to them all day.
>
> (Comments from participant LSA)

The group seized the opportunity to compare and contrast their experiences in the classroom, particularly with regard to training opportunities and collaborative working practices, which were surprisingly varied. The LSAs began to delve below the surface into the values, practices and processes of what goes on in school.

I had presumed that I was a step ahead of the LSAs in terms of 'delving and discovering' as my preliminary investigations and observations had compelled me to assess the culture of the school. I was surprised, therefore, to find that I became embroiled in *their* delving as the LSAs comments revealed yet another perspective, particularly on the culture of collaboration:

> Mrs X always asks me if I've got any new ideas that would fit in with the art topic coming up later in the term.

> I know what the class timetable is, and Mr Y puts his planning sheet for the week up on the wall but I seldom know specific tasks before the lesson and it would be nice to know in advance.

> If the class teacher would tell me a few days in advance what they were going to be doing then I'd quite happily make some games and things, but when I don't know until the start of the lesson then it's a wasted opportunity.

> Sometimes I just have no option but to sit like an observer right through the whole lesson.

> (Comments from participant LSAs)

I found that my own thinking continued to change as I learned from the LSAs. I began to recognise the subtle differences between acceptance and tolerance of roles and responsibilities that smother initiative and may lead to passivity and lack of personal development. I made several notes in my research diary, promising myself that I would change certain practices in my own classroom to permit LSAs to work more from their own initiative. Other teacher researchers focusing on the role of LSAs have reported making similar radical revisions of their own practices as collaborative research has transformed their understanding of the pivotal role of LSAs.

Exploring inclusion and the social model

The research participants explored different definitions of inclusion, established some of the differences between integration and inclusion and began to identify barriers to inclusion in the school. Initially the LSAs perceived these barriers in terms of physical access and financial constraints, thus abdicating responsibility for 'successful inclusion' to the LEA. I was disappointed but not surprised to hear the notion that 'if some children can't be integrated successfully then there's no chance of inclusion working'. I recognised the reasoning behind this view as based on a medical model of thinking which sees children's difficulties as related to their individual impairments, rather than as influenced by the social model of disability which looks at circumventing difficulties by removing social barriers (Oliver, 1990). The concept that some people were disabled more by their environment and experience of society's attitude to them than by their actual medical condition was a crucial concept to get across over the coming weeks.

Linked with the idea of the social model of disability was the idea that LSAs should foster children's independence or teach them to make choices and accept responsibility for their own learning. The LSAs initially found this difficult to accept until they were introduced to the work of activists in the disabled people's movement. Together we read and discussed excerpts from a wide range of books such as *Disabled People and Social Policy* (Oliver and Barnes, 1998) and *Disability Equality in the Classroom* (Rieser and Mason, 1990).

As sessions continued, and in the light of our collective reading, the LSAs became more conscious of insider perspectives and issues relating to human rights. They began to observe and try to understand and respond to children's learning styles in an attempt to develop inclusive learning experiences. As a result, they reported becoming more confident in their ability to adapt and change activities when the need arose, and more willing to make suggestions in the classroom.

In the year following our workshop sessions I noted that in varying degrees most of them altered their attitude towards disability, changing to an acceptance of the social model rather than the medical model. This was particularly evident in their problem-solving approach to teaching and learning, rather than the previous focus on the 'delivery' of the curriculum. Gradually we all changed our thinking, recognising that exploring effective pedagogy was probably the next important step in our shared development.

Eventually our focus shifted to broader issues concerning school culture and the extent to which it might help or hinder the shift from integration to inclusion. Originally LSAs had been concerned about the move towards inclusive education, particularly for children described as having 'multiple or profound learning difficulties'. They had doubts about the appropriateness and effectiveness of inclusive education for all children, and they had doubts about their own ability to 'deliver' it. Many felt that they were increasingly expected to take on a teaching role, to the detriment of their work as a care assistant, as the following remark shows:

> I think *caring* is the most important of my duties, you know – like mothering them, but often I'm too busy and pressurised by implementing work programmes.
>
> (Comment from participant LSA)

The *Index for Inclusion* became a valuable audit tool for establishing the culture of the school with regard to the work of support staff and generated further projects.

Evaluation of the research processes: what did the LSAs find helpful?

The LSAs described the processes involved in the workshops as sometimes 'gruelling', because ordinarily in the context of their work they were seldom expected to engage with controversial issues or formulate and justify their opinions. However, in their critical evaluation of our research journey their reflections were thought-provoking. They had begun to recognise that culture and structure in schools are interdependent, though attempts to bring about improvement in different aspects of school life by paying attention only to structural issues are not as likely to be successful as those that attempt to change culture too. Other comments revealed an emerging understanding of the complexities and possible differences in interpretation of the concept of inclusive education. The group recognised that other staff might see inclusion as yet another initiative or programme imposed from outside, to be absorbed and delivered, rather than a fundamental change in culture and practice involving a totally different value system.

The LSAs also thought some mainstream staff would see inclusion and integration as synonymous and this would mean that they would see no need to make any changes as they already had the IRU children sitting in mainstream classrooms. As Ainscow states:

> even the most pedagogically advanced methods are likely to be ineffective in the hands of those who implicitly or explicitly subscribe to a belief system that regards some students, at best, as disadvantaged and in need of fixing, or, worse, as deficient and, therefore, beyond fixing.
>
> (Farrell and Ainscow, 2002, p. 35)

We were fortunate to have access to written reports of in-school projects previously undertaken. Despite anonymity given to many quotes in reports, the LSAs found it relatively easy to guess the identity of the speakers – revealing a fixed and unwavering commitment to integration (as opposed to inclusion) persisting in some sections of the school. They were conscious of earlier comments made by themselves and other staff in which they suggested that some children might receive a better education in a special school, or that the school should not persist with integration (i.e. working in the mainstream classroom) for all children all the time. In the light of our new knowledge, a critical point in our collective learning involved facing up to our own presumptions and prejudices and understanding that there would be no simple prescription or blueprint for inclusion.

Summary of outcomes and reflections relating to the research

An important part of the research involved providing opportunities for a small group of LSAs – a group marginalized and disempowered in the traditional hierarchies of schools – to develop their understanding of values, processes and professional practices in relation to their work, through open and democratic discussion. Our discussions were an important part of every session in which participants raised questions, tested out ideas and engaged in critical debate. The 'outcomes' of the research process were ongoing as part of a process of changing understanding and attitudes. For my own part, I learned more from the group by resisting the urge to provide prompt answers to some of their questions. The growing sense of empowerment and engagement on the part of the LSAs was one development which emerged in the research experience, and this enabled them to critique the systems and values which, in the past, they had submitted or, sometimes, adhered to. As part of that critique, which involved *seeing* familiar contexts and practices in a new light and from different vantage points, members of the group discovered a heightened awareness of relationships and practices which they had previously taken for granted, as well as sharpening analytical and debating skills.

Out of the discussions held during the period of the research project, and in reviewing my records of the emergent arguments put forward in the group, a number of key ideas have begun to crystallise. First, there needs to be a culture shift within school if policies and practice are to be transformed in support of *inclusive* rather than integrated education. Information about inclusive education, and issues relating to education policy and practices, need to be disseminated and discussed at grass-roots level. Staff in school need time to reflect on their own attitudes and sometimes they will need to be challenged to consider 'inclusion' from the perspective of others, particularly the children. Learning Support Assistants recognised that it had taken them some time to examine their own feelings and attitudes towards the issues involved, and to begin to understand and assimilate new concepts. They were surprised to find policies and other documents produced at LEA and even government level (e.g. that Green Paper *Excellence for all Children*, DfEE, 1997) that they felt would necessitate major changes in schools. Although they did not feel deliberately excluded from relevant consultation, debate and training issues, they were not aware of any structures or systems that would facilitate better involvement. They recognised that many teaching staff were probably in the same situation. They recognised this is a whole-school issue, and became keen to contribute to future development plans.

Second, knowledge and understanding of the social model of disability, rather than the medical model, create new attitudes towards children described as having 'special educational needs' by shifting the responsibility for 'the problem' away from the child. Incidentally, one outcome of the project that I noted is that understanding of the social model had been carried over into other areas of practice. Some of the LSAs commented that they now found themselves more able to recognise and react to different children's learning styles – and now looked at every child's strengths, style of learning and their possible requirements, not just at the 'needs' of the children labelled as 'special'. The LSAs also realise that the problem-solving approach needs adults to find imaginative ways of creating a curriculum for success rather than one that tends to highlight failure. One of my original aims had been to raise standards and improve pupil achievement by developing the knowledge and skills of LSAs in the school in relation to classroom practice. Although at one stage I thought it an unattainable goal, I came to recognise over the coming months that my project had probably achieved this aim, but not in the way I had originally intended.

The third important observation to emerge from these projects is that it is essential to provide joint training for teachers and LSAs to enable development of effective collaborative practices based on principles of inclusion and effective use of human and other resources. The degree of collaborative working between teachers and LSAs will not increase until this training has convinced staff of the possible benefits and there is a strong whole-school commitment to making time available for it.

The research discussions suggested there were many other factors influencing the degree of collaborative working between teachers and LSAs, including: tradition, individual personalities, self-consciousness, lack of experience of managing the work of other colleagues, a feeling on the part of some teachers that their lessons should run smoothly without the need for other adult support, a belief that the LSA is there to support a particular child rather than support the teacher or the whole class in general, a feeling that support is not timetabled at the most appropriate time.

A related issue is the problem of the lack of non-contact time in primary schools which compels teachers to do most of their planning and preparation at home, so it becomes easier to give LSAs a copy of *what* will be done in the lesson than to share ideas about *how* it could be done. Some of the LSAs' contractual hours need to be devoted to planning future lessons (which includes evaluating past lessons) with teachers – although anecdotal evidence suggests that all the LSAs' contractual hours are spent working with children.

A fourth relates to professional development and training opportunities for support staff, which clearly have been very limited to date. Support staff did not *expect* to hear of training opportunities. In the absence of any demand for training, little was provided. Previous GEST and INSET budgets prioritised further training for teachers rather than support staff. Since the development of the Literacy Hour and Numeracy Hour, teaching assistants and classroom assistants have been appointed specifically to support the core curriculum areas. During the research, participants reviewed the DfEE induction course files provided for these assistants and were annoyed to find that, at the time, the course files were made available only to newly appointed support staff with particular job titles. They felt that other support staff, although quite experienced, would have benefited from the opportunity to use the induction course materials in other ways, e.g. as an audit of their skills. We commented on this to the LEA, requesting that induction course materials and trainings on the National Literacy and Numeracy frameworks should be made available to the wider group of support staff employed in schools. We were delighted to find, in the following year, that the LEA adopted the generic term LSA for all support staff, and made it quite clear in a circular to schools that trainings 'for LSAs' were now for any support staff, experienced or newly appointed, no matter what their job title or job description. Our research *had* engineered real change.

Newly introduced DfEE (2000) induction and training packages for LSAs were welcomed by members of the group, but concern was expressed about the extra work load they created for already stretched teaching staff who were then expected to act as mentors to LSAs in school. We came up with ideas for alternative ways of using these training packages, tailoring them to meet the individual needs of the larger group of support staff employed in the school. Given more time, we could have produced a programme of in-house training based on the results of earlier research into the training needs of our own staff. We did succeed in raising awareness of LSA training needs and entitlement at senior management level, so that future INSET days offered better access to training for LSAs and there was some attempt to provide equal opportunities with teaching staff. Good progress has been made in providing ICT training for support staff. Although the New Opportunity Fund training appeared to be for teachers only, the head teacher provided similar learning opportunities for most of the support staff too. The LSAs welcomed the *Good Practice Guide* (DfES, 2000) and thoroughly approved of the *Survival Guide* produced by Lorentz (1998).

On investigation we found some LEA courses that met the needs of established, more experienced staff. However, like the ones offered by local HE providers, they ran over several weeks, out of school hours, and at considerable expense to the individual. It was felt that the courses conflicted with family commitments, and that although there might be some personal satisfaction in completing them, they enhanced neither career opportunities nor salary levels.

Although the government scrapped the Individual Learning Accounts scheme that we intended to use for funding, two of our support staff did eventually obtain funding from other sources (quite independently of the school) and went on to enrol on the NVQ courses for Teaching Assistants as soon as they became available in our area. They put in a great deal of effort and commitment, in their own time and over a long period, until eventually they successfully completed the course in 2002. Although their achievement was recognised by the LEA and the school, it is probably fair to say that their increased level of skill is still not being fully utilised by the school, and to date it has not led to any improvements in career opportunities or salary levels for them.

One of the by-products of personal development on such courses is often an increase in confidence and assertiveness. The LSAs who took part in this project now look set to undertake their own action research project soon, in order to offer governors and senior management concrete suggestions for their career development and renumeration. Despite a great deal of rhetoric from the DfES about the development and promotion of 'higher level' teaching assistants there is at the time of writing no national body that can set salary levels or design a career structure according to roles and responsibilities for support staff in *all* schools. Because salary levels are still negotiated locally, we discovered anecdotal evidence of unfair practice and considerable differences between LEAs and even within schools in the same LEA. This lack of equal opportunities, or even blatant discrimination, relates to contracts and conditions of employment in addition to salary levels.

In order to develop understanding of the issues, values and practices involved in relation to inclusive education and their own contribution LSAs, like all members of the community, will need time to examine their own beliefs and feelings, and encouragement to become actively involved in the development of new policies and practices. Although training that raises awareness of specific disabilities, and teaches strategies for supporting particular pupils, could be useful, it can create the idea that LSAs (and teachers) cannot cope unless they become 'experts' in many fields. Training that raises the LSAs' confidence in their ability to adopt a problem-solving approach as part of a collaborative team is much more useful, and initially it is easier to deliver. The training needs of teaching staff were recognised within the group:

> some mainstream class teachers will need to adjust and learn to cope with children with different needs *and* extra adult support in their rooms. Some of them have always been able to delegate responsibility for certain children to other staff, and it can't carry on like that if we try to move towards an inclusive ethos.
>
> (Comments from participant LSA)

Conclusion

At the start of this chapter I mentioned that I enjoyed providing opportunities for others, and that has been one of the most rewarding outcomes of this research project. At a superficial level we all enjoyed the chance to have time away from the classroom, to do something different. Gradually it dawned upon the research participants that *they* could affect positive change and we all enjoyed the deeper levels of complex thought and communication that setting aside research time enabled us to develop over the weeks. Research participation gave all of us confidence and new skills and it set off a train of action that is still ongoing over a year later. We made the time for research which enabled new relationships and alliances. We found it tiring yet incredibly stimulating as we developed new thinking and practice. As we go on to work with other staff I see the ripples of recognition slowly spreading the message of inclusion quietly and unobtrusively, yet far more effectively than I could have imagined. It leaves me with a feeling of satisfaction in a job well done, and a few ideas for new projects beginning to surface!

References

Balshaw, M. (1991) *Help in the Classroom,* London: David Fulton.

Bell, F. (1988) 'Support of mainstreamed children with special education needs by non-teaching assistants', *British Psychological Society Division of Educational and Child Psychology Newsletter* 29, 28–31.

Booth, T., Ainscow, M., Black-Hawkins, K., Vaughan, M. and Shaw, L. (2002) *Index for Inclusion*, Manchester: Centre for Studies on Inclusive Education.

Clayton, T. (1989a) 'The role and management of welfare assistants', in T. Bowers (ed.) *Managing Special Needs*, Buckingham: Open University Press.

Clayton, T. (1989b) 'The role of welfare assistants in supporting children with Special Educational Needs in ordinary primary schools', in R. Evans (ed.) *Response to Special Educational Needs,* Oxford: Blackwell.

Clayton, T. (1990a) 'Welfare assistants: are they equipped for their role?' *Support for Learning* 5 (4), 193–8.

Clayton, T. (1990b) 'The training needs of special welfare assistants: what do Heads, class teachers and assistants regard as important?' *Educational and Child Psychology* 7 (1), 44–51.

Clayton, T. (1993) 'Welfare assistants in the classroom: problems and solutions', *Educational Psychology in Practice* 8 (4), 191–7.

DfEE (1997) *Excellence for all Children: Meeting Special Educational Needs*, London: Stationery Office.

DfEE (1998) *Meeting Special Educational Needs: Programme of Action*, London: Department for Education and Employment.

DfEE (2000) *Teaching Assistant File: Induction Training for Teaching Assistants*, London: Department for Education and Employment.

DfES (2000) *Working with Teaching Assistants: a Good Practice Guide*, London: Department for Education and Skills.

Farrell, P. and Ainscow, M. (2002) *Making Special Education Inclusive,* London: David Fulton.

Farrell, P., Balshaw, M. and Polat, F. (2000) *The Management, Role and Training of Learning Support Assistants*, London: Department for Education and Employment.

Fox, G. (1993) *A Handbook for Special Needs Assistants,* London: David Fulton.

Lorenz, S. (1996) *Supporting Support Assistants,* Bury: Bury Professional Development Centre.

Lorenz, S. (1998) *The Support Assistant's Survival Guide,* Bury: Bury Professional Development Centre.

O'Brien, T. and Garner, P. (eds) (2001) *Untold Stories: Learning Support Assistants and their Work*, Stoke on Trent: Trentham Books.

Oliver, M. (1990) *The Politics of Disablement,* London: Macmillan.

Oliver, M. and Barnes, C. (1998) *Disabled People and Social Policy*, London: Longman.

Rieser, R. and Mason, M. (1990) *Disability Equality in the Classroom: a Human Rights Issue,* London: Disability Equality in Education.

TTA (1998) *National Standards for Special Educational Needs Co-ordinators*, Nottingham: Teacher Training Agency.

TTA (1999) *National SEN Specialist Standards,* Nottingham: Teacher Training Agency.

Woolf, M. and Bassett, S. (1988) 'How classroom assistants respond', *British Journal for Special Education* 15 (2), 62–4.

Chapter 5

Students who challenge

Reducing barriers to inclusion

Linda Simpson

This chapter explores a multi-dimensional approach to practitioner research and reflects on how the outcomes from a small-scale project can help to build and develop a collaborative, problem-solving approach to reducing barriers to inclusion. Inclusive education, however, is not a 'quick fix' (Corbett, 2001). Real change takes time and the move towards an inclusive community presents many challenges for schools. We are, in my own school (an 11–18 comprehensive), at the beginning of an exploration into our culture, ethos and practice from which we can develop inclusive policies. This action research project forms only one small element in the move towards this goal.

We are on the brink of a detailed self-review, using the *Index for Inclusion* (Ainscow and Booth, 2002) as a framework. Action research will provide an additional strand in finding out more about the school from both 'macro' and 'micro' levels and help to deepen our knowledge and understanding of individual learners.

Much of my work as a Learning Support Co-ordinator involves critical reflection and evaluation through a process not dissimilar to the cyclical nature of action research, involving identification, planning, implementation and review and aiming to improve practice by 'trying to induce beneficial change' (Bassey, 1995, p. 6). As a practitioner with a whole-school brief, I feel action research could be a very powerful and influential catalyst for change.

Arguably some of the biggest barriers to learning and participation are related to issues of challenging behaviour, and this is certainly the case in my own school and many others. Corbett raises the difficult question 'Is including children with challenging behaviours an inclusion too far?' (Corbett, 2001, p. 27).

The issues, understandings, perceptions and arguments surrounding the inclusion of this varied group of children are very wide-ranging and vary from context to context. How, for example, could challenging behaviour be defined within my own school? Could I assume there is a shared understanding among staff and how could 'connective pedagogies' best be developed to facilitate and support the inclusion of these children? Connective pedagogy is about identifying and linking flexible, responsive approaches with teaching and learning which not only recognise the way individuals learn best and how individual learning styles are linked with the curriculum but also connect values, experiences and relationships both within school and with the wider community (Corbett, 2001, p. 1). Connective pedagogy also 'extends' to 'emotional literacy, to understanding the connections between our feelings, our reasoning and our motivation' (Corbett, 2001, p. 115).

The challenge as I saw it was to view the research project from a three-dimensional focus as described by Corbett (2001, p. 31). A dimension which involves and results in strategic planning and the practicalities of implementing an intervention plan. A dimension which extends into the wider community, and the values inherent in the community and a dimension that probes inside the self and both questions and challenges understandings, beliefs and values, as part of a wider examination of the school culture.

The Learning Centre

With behaviour chosen as the area for research and the multi-dimensional approach as the focus, I identified the Learning Support Unit within college as the context. The unit, or Learning Centre as it is known, opened in September 2002, initially funded by the government's Standards Fund for on-site units. It is based within an 11–18 comprehensive school situated on a city housing estate with a high level of social and economic need. The centre forms part of the support framework within school and offers a part-time placement for students at risk of exclusion. Students are admitted on a short-term basis (six weeks) and are organised according to year groups of no more than six members. They attend on a part-time basis to enable continued access to the curriculum areas they enjoy or are achieving success in. They follow the curriculum in subjects they are withdrawn from, and teaching is adapted to suit the individual learning styles of the students as far as possible. Learning is at the centre of the programme and though protocols have been agreed the system is very flexible. Subject and pastoral staff are included in the planning and delivery of programmes and 'reintegration' is an integral part of the planning process. Corbett describes what she sees as 'connectedness' for teachers though, and also summarises well what we are aiming to provide for the students, 'to feel able to connect into support systems which are flexible, non-judgemental' and a safe space 'in which to explore challenges and barriers without blame' (Corbett, 2001, p. 116).

The existence of such units inevitably raises difficult questions concerning inclusion and exclusion and creates dilemmas for schools such as mine. How, for example, can inclusive values and policies be formed and established in a community that provides what could arguably be seen as segregated, exclusive provision within the school community itself? The senior managers in school were very aware of these dilemmas and were committed to establishing the centre as an integral part of what they deemed to be the 'continuum of provision' within the school and to involve all staff in the planning and preparation. As Learning Support Co-ordinator I was asked to co-ordinate the planning and to manage the centre once it was in operation.

As an initial step I set up a steering group to identify the aims of the centre, admission and exit criteria, programme planning, the reintegration process and ways in which students, parents and staff could be involved in these processes. The group included senior managers, pastoral heads and support services and met over the course of two terms prior to the opening of the centre, and a multi-agency group, or co-ordinating group, now meets termly to offer support, discuss issues and monitor the working of the centre. We recognised the importance of evaluating the impact of the centre itself and identified a number of questions for further exploration:

- How do we identify the specific difficulties experienced by students admitted to the centre?
- What are the barriers to learning?
- What baseline data would be most useful to inform planning, target setting and monitoring?
- How do we monitor students' progress and their participation in mainstream classes during placement?
- Has attendance in the centre helped to reduce any barriers to learning and participation?

In particular, we wanted to explore these questions in ways which involved the students, parents and their teachers not only to inform the areas under scrutiny but also to support the reintegration process and to help subject staff to consider and reflect on approaches and strategies in their own practice for including these students in their classrooms. The overall aim of the research was to identify and develop a more co-ordinated, collaborative and supportive approach to the inclusion of students with challenging behaviour.

The multi-agency group was involved in identifying the focus of the research project, but a smaller core group was involved in planning, implementing and evaluating the intervention. The core group consisted of the Learning Centre Co-ordinator, link Learning Support Assistant and myself as Learning Support Co-ordinator.

The second cohort of students from Year 10 was admitted to the Learning Centre at the beginning of term. The research was carried out during their six-week placement and during the reintegration programme. I used a cyclical model (Elliot, 1991; Bassey, 1995) as a framework for planning, implementing, gathering data and evaluating the research.

I reflected on Bassey's fundamental questions when embarking on this study. What do you seek to know that you didn't know before, and why? How will this change the world? In response to the last question, I think it is important in a small-scale project such as this to have realistic expectations. I did not intend to change the world but aimed to make a difference and move towards the development of a more inclusive, connective pedagogy.

Action research and collaboration

Action research should not be viewed as a 'neat problem-solving process' but rather as a 'constant process of asking further and more interesting questions about practice' (Green, 2002, p. 130). Green describes action research as 'fundamentally exploratory' (2002, p. 126). In this section I begin to explore the research from a wider perspective.

This was not, of course, a piece of research carried out in isolation. It is important to recognise that both within the core group and the wider group of colleagues involved there were potential tensions and dilemmas, similar to those referred to by Elliot (1991) as 'a clash of professional values' between traditional pedagogy and reflective practice. This highlights the importance of dialogue and collaboration in all aspects of the research, including concepts and ideas based on theory. Collaboration is seen as an essential element in the development of an inclusive culture (Kuglemass, 2001; Carrington and Elkins, 2002). Building relationships and shared approaches are therefore crucial and a failure to achieve them may present some of the biggest barriers to the development of a 'connective pedagogy'. Certainly within my own school community there is a predominantly traditionalist approach to pedagogy with a focus on content and the 'transmission' of knowledge and a mixed commitment to inclusive education which will require supportive systems and structures through which to evolve more collaborative processes.

What are the wider issues relating to the inclusion of young people identified as experiencing social, emotional and behavioural difficulties and what impact do these have within my own context?

Hargreaves (1999) emphasises the rift in cultures within schools in which 'more and more children belong to cultures that are different and unfamiliar to those of the teachers', a situation which Bigum and Green (1993) describe students as often being seen as 'aliens in the classroom'. The values, expectations, language and behaviour of the students and their families from the wider community my own school serves can be very different from those promoted by the dominant culture within the school. This is a central issue for the development of inclusive school communities and it raises a number of important questions within my own context, particularly in relation to students presenting challenging behaviours who are often seen as 'different beings'. How 'connective' are we with 'cultural factors' and to what extent do we expect the students to 'fit in' (Corbett, 2001, p. 117)? This research and future work have to reflect on these crucial issues and to consider further how we can develop a 'depth of emotional understanding' from which we can begin to build these bridges.

The research

In the introduction I referred to the multi-dimensional approach adopted in the research project, an approach which incorporates a variety of dimensions and enables the research questions to be considered from a number of different perspectives. The strategies used for gathering data were therefore carefully selected to ensure that the focus was not only on the students and staff from the centre, but set within a wider context. The methods used and subsequent evaluations were, of course, influenced by my own reflections. Indeed, Elliot views these two aspects – action and reflection – as strands in a single process (1991). This process, as outlined in my initial plan, was constantly moving and changing and can be seen as a 'spiral of cycles' in which the 'general idea is allowed to shift' (Elliot, 1991, p. 70).

Approaching this project from an ethical stance, I started by consulting all participants to seek consent, outline the research brief, discuss issues of confidentiality and arrangements for feedback. Bassey describes these ethical principles as 'respect for persons, truth and democratic principles' (1995, p. 21), but they may also create tensions within the research process, as they depend on openness centred on 'critical debate', which involves exposure or 'scrutiny' of weaknesses as well as strengths in existing pedagogies. The importance of talk, open dialogue, listening and mutual respect is worth re-emphasising as essential elements in such a process. These dilemmas are clearly evident and present particular challenges within my own school. This underlines collaboration as a key element in change. I found Fullan's words particularly thought-provoking in relation to these dilemmas:

> Don't assume that your version of what the change should be is the one that could or should be implemented. You have to exchange your reality of what should be through interaction with others concerned.
>
> (Cited in Robson, 2002, p. 220)

In my research diary I raised the question 'How can staff be engaged in talk and "critical debate" and is it necessary to involve all?' Fullan argues not, but I feel there surely needs to be a 'critical mass' for change to be implemented?

With both the focus of my research and ethical principles in mind, a 'general plan' was drawn up following a meeting with the core group. This included the range of approaches outlined in Table 5.1. I kept a research diary throughout the research process. It became essential for recording developments in the research and my own thoughts and observations.

Table 5.1 General plan

Date	Activity	Monitoring	Duration	Comments
27 Jan – 14 Feb	Clarifying the general idea	Research diary	Two weeks	Team meeting (LC co-ordinator, link LSA).
	'Reconnaissance'	Gathering baseline data		Discuss and negotiate activities with all
	Action research proposal	Initial interviews/ observation Target setting	One week	involved. Formulation of plan. Data
	First action step			already available – co-ordinators' interviews with parents and students. Profiles from subject staff
17 Feb	Half-term			
24 Feb – 14 March	Implementation of plan	Diaries – research and student	Daily	Team meeting to discuss first action step, plan for next action
		Observations	One or two lessons per student per week	and any revision/ modifications
		Interviews with staff and parents	One day	Conducted during prearranged review (week 7)
		Shadow study		
17–28 March	Reintegration programme	Observation	One reintegration lesson	Feedback to staff Team meeting
		Student/staff interviews		
		Profiles		
		Data analysis/ evaluation		
		Write up research report		

Baseline data were gathered from a variety of sources, including profiles of students completed by subject staff prior to entry. These profiles had been discussed at the initial core group meeting, as information from subject teachers was felt to be a crucial part of the process in identifying barriers. Nevertheless, we had to be sensitive to the fact that these provided the perspectives of teachers involved rather than those of the students. With this in mind semi-structured interviews were carried out with both the students being admitted to the centre and their parents by the centre co-ordinator. It was intended that these would be completed at both the start and end of the placement, though difficulties in communicating with parents as well as staff absence resulted in only initial interviews being carried out within the time scale of the initial project.

Observations were conducted throughout the six-week placement, though once again the time scale was difficult to keep to and highlighted the need to carefully consider and balance not only the research action and the questions we were seeking to explore, but also current systems and practice in relation to the time frame and intended aims of the centre.

It was intended that as part of the initial gathering of baseline data in class observations on all six students would be carried out by the specialist teacher using a continuous, non-participant observation technique. This would not only help us to form a fuller picture of barriers to learning, but would also provide valuable insights into aspects of teaching and learning and would help us to identify focus areas for individual planning. I quickly realised that I needed to keep in focus a sense of what could be realistically achieved in what amounted to only a few weeks for the initial 'stage'.

In consultation with the team, therefore, the decision was made to focus on one student, Christopher, for the initial observation and later study. Though this would not provide such a broad picture from the outset in relation to all students, it would allow me to probe and explore in depth some of the research issues. This had to be rethought yet again, however, as, owing to very difficult family circumstances, Christopher was not attending school on a regular basis. It was agreed that general observations would continue to form part of the action plan, though these would be carried out during the implementation period and another student would be identified (Michael) as the focus of the shadow study. It is worth noting an entry in my diary during this time:

> Finding the time for an observation is extremely difficult. Each time this has been arranged, Michael is absent, has absconded, a supply teacher is taking the lesson or I have been put on the cover rota!

The shadow study was used as a means of in-depth monitoring following a general observation. The centre co-ordinator carried this out over two days (following discussion and consultation with staff concerned) as a means of providing data not only on the aspects of behaviour identified, in this case 'on task/off task' behaviour, but also responses and interactions within different learning contexts at different times of the day. It was also used as a means of initiating discussion on teaching styles and approaches to learning. A recording schedule was drawn up for the purpose of the study.

Staff and student interviews were conducted during the reintegration phase. Once again these were semi-structured and aimed not only to provide data for the research, but also to stimulate discussion and help to evaluate outcomes. Five teachers from different curriculum areas took part.

Student perspectives

Two students were asked to keep diaries during the placement. I felt that it was important to include the insights, reflections and views of the students throughout the research. 'Students represent hidden voices who, if listened to, may assist in making schools and classrooms more inclusive' (Ainscow et al., 1999, p. 139). It is so easy to overlook or simply pay lip service to these voices and I think both within my own school and in education generally we need to reflect on how we listen if we are to create environments where students are able to take control of their own learning. In other words we need to learn from the learner. The approach was very open and, on reflection, I feel that much more guidance and perhaps structure were needed, for a number of reasons.

It was an entirely new and unfamiliar task for both students. Personal organisation was not a strength of either and diaries were often 'misplaced'. It would have been useful to perhaps have continual dialogue running along-side the diaries to enable them to give verbal entries and to discuss more fully some of their views and perceptions. The data from these diaries are at best patchy and in parts very personal. For these reasons I will not be including the data in the analysis. However, it is worth noting some of the central issues that emerged from the diaries and interviews, though of course these will be my own personal interpretations of the students' perspectives and responses.

Relations with staff were highlighted a number of times, with mutual respect and the ability to listen being key qualities, reflected in their views on subjects they could access or felt included in. The relevance of the curriculum on offer was also a major issue in the participation of some students and, I would argue, underlines the focus on content and outcomes that excludes and marginalises these students. The differences in culture I discussed previously were evident in the students' views on the value and expectations of the school, the opportunities provided by education, and their aspirations beyond it. These interpretations are, of course, based on the perspectives of a very small group of students but nevertheless I feel they do provide a useful insight into culture and practice and reinforce the importance of listening seriously to student voices in the process of developing an inclusive school.

Research outcomes: context, interpretation and analysis

My interpretation of the data was inevitably influenced by my own values, and beliefs and actions can be interpreted in many different ways. Bassey describes this process as a 'complex tangle of beliefs, aims, methods, language and intellectual structures' (1995, p. 4). The challenge for me was to try and make sense of it, not just to consider what it meant for me personally but to look at how it could contribute to developing a more inclusive culture of teaching and learning within school.

First, and I think an important factor in the way the research evolved, was that others have been involved not just as participants, but also as researchers. There were a number of advantages and disadvantages in conducting small-scale research with such a group. It provided an established forum for open discussions specifically relating to the focus of the research and also provided opportunities for much wider reflections. We had previously agreed what we understood to be the guiding principles of the centre and the overall aims of the research and were able to discuss, albeit briefly at times, on a daily basis any issues or concerns that arose. This helped to minimise any differences or tensions within the group. It also presented difficulties, however, as the planning, implementation and collection of data relied on all of the group being able to complete actions within the time frame. In addition, there were many variables (attendance, social issues and time constraints) beyond my control which affected the research process and resulted at times in much frustration and inevitable modification of the plan. This reflects, however, the reality of a real school context in which responsiveness and flexibility are essential (Robson, 2002).

The first evaluation of the action research process followed the initial 'action step'. At the first core group meeting it became clear from the data gathered that although it provided some valuable information and insights into specific areas of difficulty, there were some additional questions we needed to ask regarding this process. When should the process begin and what exactly were we looking for? The students had already started their placement and we were still gathering baseline data, not a good starting point, as the questions relating to difficulties and barriers needed to be examined to inform the planning. Clearly the time frame in the future projects will need to include a pre-admission period for gathering baseline information. We also needed to address the first two research questions in this period. We were trying to identify specific difficulties experienced by individual students, as well as barriers to learning, including teaching and learning styles and the extent to which the curriculum on offer influences behaviour. Learning theories may help us to better understand what is happening within the classroom.

I have previously mentioned the predominantly traditionalist pedagogy within my own context, with strong roots in the 'transmission' approach. This traditional model of teaching 'imposes restrictions on change' (Carrington and Elkins, 2002, p. 3). Should we not be developing a model of learning, which takes account of cultural influences outside the college (emphasised by Bruner) and includes the ideas of the constructivist theorists like Bruner and Vygotsky? These surely will enable us to understand better, and value more, individual learners and what they bring to the learning process – a student-focused culture rather than content-led curriculum. This would also help us to develop a stronger emotional understanding of these students, a concept I explored earlier which, as I develop my own thinking on pedagogy, assumes a pivotal role not only within the context of my own research but within the wider college community. Corbett supports this view: 'An effectively inclusive school is one which values emotional literacy, as this is one of the ways in which the curriculum can be truly responsive to difference' (Corbett, 2001, p. 104).

I have mentioned the importance of collaboration with parents. Florian and Rouse (2001) found that extensive work with parents was one of the main characteristics of schools identified as successful in their approach to inclusive education. The support offered in the Learning Centre was certainly seen very positively by the parents. It proved very difficult, however, to engage some of the parents even for initial interviews and it was clear from the first action step that we needed to consider how we communicated with and engaged parents in the work of the centre. The parental interviews did, however, provide perspectives on behaviour, which we were able to compare and contrast with college and student perspectives, and this helped us to identify particular areas of difficulty. The interview format and structure were modified to include shared planning and targets, and ways of developing links were identified. The information also highlighted the importance of sharing the collation of information, analysis and planning. The responsibility for all of this had largely been within the role of the Learning Centre co-ordinator. We decided that in future we would form a core team with key personnel for each cohort to help meet one of the aims of the research, the gathering of essential baseline data.

The observations that were carried out during this time provided a lot of information on responses and behaviours within the classroom. Their purpose being to 'gain an insight into the child, teacher, learning environment and complex interaction between them' (Fairhurst, 2000, p. 98). This was also the premise on which we based the shadow study. The outcomes were difficult to interpret, however, and responses varied enormously. A lot of variables were considered, such as structure, pace, content, type of activities, interaction and timing. We compared them with other data such as teacher and student interviews. Interestingly the observer (also the co-ordinator) concluded that Michael's responses reflected the value he put on the subjects. Michael, in academic assessment terms, is identified as of at least 'average ability' and resources used in the lesson certainly present no barriers for him. This does raise a further question about the use and meaning of the concept 'ability' and what criteria and methods we use to categorise students in this way.

The interviews were conducted with five subject staff, which provided a lot of valuable data and an opportunity for discussion with colleagues. All but one of the staff interviewed were willing to explore a collaborative teaching approach. This also raised a number of questions. Could a culture of reflective practice be developed through such action research projects as this one? Are individual differences being viewed as challenges rather than obstacles? Could the communication, dialogue and more open approach developed through the research lead to a commitment to 'collaborative problem solving' highlighted by Ainscow (in Corbett, 2001, p. 26)? Whatever the reasons, I did see this as a step towards positive change.

Interestingly, though not surprisingly, my initial assumption that staff had a shared understanding of challenging behaviour proved false. All the behaviours described as challenging by these teachers were different and ranged from use of language and non-compliance to verbal and physical aggression. Perhaps one starting point in evolving collaborative approaches could be the development of a shared understanding of this complex issue. These approaches I see as practices, which have clear goals, understood and supported by teachers, who are actively seeking to remove barriers to learning through creating an environment more responsive to individual needs.

Reflections and conclusion

In many ways the critical analysis of the research project presents the greatest challenge. How could I begin to summarise the process itself, draw conclusions from it, reflect on what it has meant for me and state what claims to changes and improvement towards inclusive pedagogy could be made, particularly in relation to challenging behaviour?

The research certainly enabled me to reflect on my own assumptions, beliefs and values and those of my colleagues and the school as a whole. It has not only challenged these by exploring the various dimensions of the project from different perspectives, but has also provided a clear focus and framework from which to explore a range of issues surrounding the ways in which barriers to inclusion can be reduced by focusing on the development of connective pedagogies, rather than primarily on 'bad behaviour'.

The actual process involved in being a teacher-researcher has certainly impacted on my thinking. It has helped to give me a greater understanding and insight into pedagogy and confirmed my belief in the importance of valuing individual learners and in recognising the influence social and cultural factors have on curriculum and pedagogy. It has taken me out of the 'comfort zone' as both teacher and learner and forced me to rethink many previously held assumptions in ways that challenge my own practice and the practices within school.

There were many positive experiences and outcomes from the research, but my feelings throughout were mixed, mirrored by those described by Strauss as unsettling and disturbing (in Day *et al.*, 2002, p. 221). Like Strauss, it was the issues raised by the research surrounding pedagogy that unsettled me the most and raised some very challenging questions not just for me personally but for the school community as a whole. How can we develop inclusive pedagogies within a culture that is so different and, arguably, distant from the community it serves? How do we develop an ethos and establish principles which value and respect individual differences? How do we effect real change when many are resistant to it? How do we establish a culture in which talking, listening, collaboration and respect underpin practice? These are some very challenging, fundamental issues and underline how crucial it is to view action research as an 'ongoing professional commitment' through which greater understanding and insight on such issues can be reached (Bassey, 1995, p. 47).

Was the overall aim of the research achieved, and to what extent were the research questions answered? It was when I was reflecting on this that Corbett's view of measuring effectiveness in terms of quality assurance seemed particularly relevant to my own research. It is all about 'assessing the quality of student experience' and how as a school we 'respond to individual need' (Corbett, 2001, p. 95). We have, I feel, through the actions implemented, just begun to explore in depth the questions raised from a number of perspectives and in doing so have not only improved practice within the boundaries of our focus, but identified other questions, which will form an integral part in the process of transforming culture and practice in the school. These questions are, however, open-ended, in that there are no definitive or easy answers and we will need to continue revisiting them as a 'measure of quality learning'.

As a result of the research, we have as a team developed new approaches, systems, practices and an evaluation framework that we would argue provide a more co-ordinated, collaborative approach but which we see as the beginning of and only a part of an evolving process.

This is a process that crosses traditional boundaries in teaching. It is about a holistic approach, a 'connective pedagogy' (Corbett, 2001) and 'blended services' (Carrington and Elkins, 2002), underpinned by a constructivist curriculum, centred around the knowledge, personal history and culture of the students. The place of voice and listening is, of course, central to this process and I think we are only at the very beginning, in our school, of exploring and finding ways of ensuring not only that we hear the voices of the students, their parents and the community, but that we take them seriously. This process also has at its core emotional understanding and collaboration, based on respect, openness to critical debate and reflection through which more inclusive approaches to difference can be explored.

References

Ainscow, M., Booth, T. and Dyson, A. (1999) 'Inclusion and exclusion in schools: listening to some hidden voices', in K. Ballard (ed.) *Inclusive Education: International Voices on Disability and Justice*, London: Falmer.

Bassey, M. (1995) *Creating Education through Research*, Newark: Kirklington Moor Press.

Bigum, C. and Green, B. 'Aliens in the classroom', *Australian Journal of Education* 37 (2), 119–41.

Carrington, S. and Elkins, J. (2002) 'Comparisons of a traditional and an inclusive secondary school culture', *International Journal of Inclusive Education* 6 (1), 1–16.

Corbett, J. (2001) *Supporting Inclusive Education: a Connective Pedagogy*, London: Falmer Press.

Day, C., Elliott, J., Somekh, B. and Winter, R. (eds) (2002) *Theory and Practice in Action Research*, Oxford: Symposium Books.

Elliott, J. (1991) *Action Research for Educational Change*, Buckingham: Open University Press.

Fairhurst, P. (ed.) (2000) *Planning for Positive Behaviour*, Carlisle: Cumbria County Council.

Florian, L. and Rouse, M. (2001) 'Achieving high standards and the inclusion of pupils with special educational needs', *Cambridge Journal of Education* 31 (3).

Green, K. (2002) 'Defining the field of literature in action research: a personal approach', in C. Day, J. Elliot, B. Somekits and R. Winter (eds) *Theory and Practice in Action Research*. Oxford: Symposium Books.

Hargreaves, A. (1999) *Emotional Geographies of Teaching*, Perth WA: Chalkface Press.

Kugelmass, J. (2001) 'Collaboration and compromise in creating and sustaining an inclusive school', *International Journal of Inclusive Education* 5 (1), 47–65.

Robson, C. (2002) *Real World Research*, Oxford: Blackwell.

Verkuyten, M. (2002) 'Making teachers accountable for students' disruptive classroom behaviour', *British Journal of Society of Education* 23 (1), 107–22.

Visser, J., Cole, T. and Daniels, H. (2002) 'Inclusion for the difficult to include', *Support for Learning* 17 (1), 23–6.

Vulliamy, G. and Webb, R. (1993) 'Special educational needs: from disciplinary to pedagogic research', *Disability Handicap and Society* 8 (2), 187–202.

Vulliamy, G. and Webb, R. (2001) 'The social construction of school exclusion rates: implications for evaluation methodology', *Educational Studies* 27 (3), 357–70.

Vulliamy, G. and Webb, R. (2003) 'Reducing school exclusions: an evaluation of a multi-site development project', *Oxford Review of Education* 29 (1), 187–202.

Further reading

Armstrong, F. (1998) 'The curriculum as alchemy: school and the struggle for cultural space', *Curriculum Studies* 6 (2), 145–60.

Blythman, M., MacLeod, D. and Cresla, M. (1989) *Classroom Observations from Inside*, Edinburgh: Spotlights SCRE, on-line at www.scre.ac.uk/index.html.

Bryant, I. (1996) 'Action, research and reflective practice', in D. Scott and R. Usher (eds) *Understanding Educational Research*, London: Routledge.

Clark, C., Dyson, A., Millward, A. and Robson, S. (1999) 'Inclusive education and schools as organisations', *International Journal of Inclusive Education* 3 (1), 37–52.

Dodds, M. and Hart, S. (2001) *Doing Practitioner Research Differently*, London: Routledge Falmer.

Eleni, S. Didaskalou and Millward, A. (2002) 'Breaking the policy log-jam: comparative perspectives on policy formulation and development for pupils with emotional and behavioural difficulties', *Oxford Review of Education* 28 (1), 109–21.

Holt, J. (2002) 'Learning to be "stupid"?' in A. Pollard (ed.) *Readings for Reflective Teaching*, London: Continuum.

Lindsay, G. (2003) 'Inclusive education: a critical perspective', *British Journal of Special Educational Needs* 30 (1), 3–12.

MacLeod, F. (2001) 'Towards inclusion: our shared responsibility for disaffected pupils', *British Journal of Special Educational Needs* 28 (4), 191–4.

McSherry, J. (2001) *Challenging Behaviour in Mainstream Schools*, London: Fulton.

QCA (2001) *Supporting school improvement. Emotional and behavioural development*, London: Qualifications and Curriculum Authority.

Tilstone, C. (1995) *Observation Skills in Unit 5 Assessment and Observations*, Birmingham: University of Birmingham.

Chapter 6

'We like to talk and we like someone to listen'

Cultural difference and minority voices as agents of change

Mary Clifton

Educational strategies and guidance are often developed by applying 'expertise' and particular kinds of knowledge in accordance with established 'good practice' from a professional perspective. How inclusive are those strategies from the perspective of the pupils? Educationalists committed to equality and to widening participation constantly strive to encourage the development of an 'inclusive ethos and curriculum' within schools, but what does this actually mean? Inclusion within the education system must not only support every pupil's basic human right to education but also ensure that each pupil feels that education to be accessible and relevant to them and that their cultural and linguistic identity is valued. Booth suggests that inclusion involves the wider community, cultures and identities, and acceptance of the value and diversity of pupils. He argues that inclusion, and thereby participation, in the education system is more than simply access to education:

> It [participation] implies learning alongside others and collaborating with them in shared lessons. It involves active engagement with what is learnt and taught and having a say in how education is experienced. But participation also involves being recognised for oneself and being accepted for oneself: I participate with you when you recognise me as a person like yourself and accept me for who I am.
>
> (Booth, 2003, p. 2)

Pupils' individual identities need to be reflected in the school environment and the curriculum, and the diversity of students' lives and cultures celebrated as an enriching resource for schools and the communities to which they belong.

The small research project discussed here took place in 'Homesvale'. The local education authority is made up of a metropolitan borough which consists of nine towns with an overall population of over 370,000. The largest town, 'Carketown' (population 120,000) is in the southern part of the borough, flanked by three smaller rural townships which make up the most affluent part of the area. The northern part of the borough has five small industrial towns, which are closely linked geographically and historically. The LEA has a pupil population of over 64,000 and within its schools there is a minority ethnic population of 25 per cent. Sixty-nine schools have percentages of minority ethnic pupils which are high enough to attract funding from the Ethnic Minority Achievement Grant (EMAG) and have trained additional staff in school working to support all minority ethnic pupils 'at risk of underachievement'. There are seventeen additional schools with significantly growing numbers of minority ethnic pupils who are supported by Ethnic Minority Achievement (EMA) Advisers and Consultants from the LEA central team. All other schools are supported on a request basis. Teacher Co-ordinators support a small number of Traveller pupils and around 230 pupils in LEA schools who are refugees or seeking asylum. In the past two years we have had an increased number of requests from schools to support pupils from many other countries who have come to live in the area for a variety of reasons. These pupils are often linguistically isolated in that no one in their family speaks English and no one in the area, or school, speaks their language. I work as an EMA consultant and one of my responsibilities is for the support and induction of what are described as 'isolated learners' into school.

In principle all these pupils have an equal right to education and we have a duty and a commitment to make that education as accessible as possible. In order to maintain the level of support that schools require we decided to develop a document with the purpose of providing effective guidance and promoting strategies for the inclusion of 'isolated learners' into the education system.

Overview of the project

In this chapter I will explore one aspect of a participatory action research project concerning how the involvement of marginalised voices was used as a contributory factor in developing and managing change. I will explore that process of change and how these seldom heard voices influenced the perceptions of systems and strategies, which led to the development of an LEA policy and guidance document for use in schools.

The initial process of talking, often informally, to colleagues and those concerned with the focus area of the research was crucial in terms of raising questions and defining the purpose and parameters of the project. In addition, these discussions helped to ensure data collection and evaluation were manageable and set within practical time limitations.

The nature of this research project involved more than simply facilitating and planning action, which can then be transformed into a written guidance document. It also involved the investigation of cultural beliefs and perceptions and the way they interact with professional practices. In this case the LEA as the (powerful) 'outsider' is involved as part of a commitment to enhancing the experience of education for all, including staff development. The action taken as a consequence of reflection on the situation is important. Henry and Kemmis (1985) also suggest that outsiders can provide 'legitimising rituals' which give recognition and status to what is achieved, in this case facilitating the participation of seldom heard voices.

Our team started out to simply review the literature produced by other LEAs and amalgamate what we considered to be the best features and practices of each. We wanted to produce a guidance document which would seek to ensure that pupils are not marginalised, and that they are provided with the best situation to facilitate their learning. I needed to consider whether the guidance we were constructing met the requirements and aspirations as perceived by pupils themselves. What are the pupils' priorities? Surely these considerations are prime ones if we accept that optimal learning conditions exist only when the learner feels safe and accepted as an equal.

'Isolated learners'

The welcome and support given to learners, who may be culturally and linguistically isolated, by schools in the LEA have been generally very positive, but they are varied. In many cases pupils and staff have welcomed new arrivals, responding to the language, learning and social needs of the pupil and celebrating the diversity of culture and languages in their school. However, although the Teacher Co-ordinator for Refugee and Asylum Seeker pupils is notified when children come to live in Homesvale, other pupils may be absorbed into the education system without schools notifying the authority. Schools or parents alert us only when a 'problem' is perceived or support required for newly arrived students.

The effectiveness of the induction period can be monitored from the perspective of a professional, but we have very little evidence other than apocryphal anecdotes about how pupils themselves perceive their school. This raises questions about the assumptions and practices of our services and support systems. We recognise that the support and resources we provide are patchy. Bilingual resources are difficult to find in some minority languages and may take weeks to arrive from the publisher or book supplier. Often pupils are placed in schools where there are no specialist EMA teachers or support staff. When schools give a positive welcome, we are able to place children in schools very quickly. Our initial aim of providing part-time support for the first four to six weeks after admission into school to facilitate a smooth induction faced difficulties. Finding appropriate bilingual classroom support assistants can be extremely difficult and, in addition, the stricter regulations pertaining to police checks mean that a pupil could be in school for weeks or months before a bilingual curriculum support assistant can be provided. It is against this background that the process of policy writing and the development of LEA guidance on strategies for induction and access to the curriculum for schools, especially those without specialist EMA staff, have been initiated.

Differences between primary and secondary experience

It was evident, on the basis of my observations and discussions with colleagues, that the secondary schools needed greater support, both for their 'isolated' pupils and for their teachers, than the primary schools. Much of the guidance published by LEAs is very similar and represents, in principal, good strategies and procedures for admission as well as advice for teachers, with examples of good classroom practice. There is an abundance of practical activities for primary pupils but less for those pupils of secondary age. The systems, cultures and practices in primary and secondary education differ. Instruction and explanation in a primary classroom are often more visual and practical than in a secondary classroom, where many teachers rely more on 'chalk and talk' to get their teaching points and instructions across. The teaching styles of primary teachers lend themselves more readily to the needs of learners new to English and to the education system.

During a consultation meeting with EMA Co-ordinators (all secondary practitioners) in which I hoped to draw on their expertise and good practice, it emerged that some felt a ready-made pack of worksheets was necessary in order to alleviate the need for mainstream teachers to differentiate the curriculum for one pupil. Such a view did not support the development of inclusive practice if individual pupils at various stages of English language acquisition were going to be fully and equitably included in lessons. A real danger in introducing a free-standing work pack is that pupils might be left to work alone and with few opportunities for interacting or discussing their work with their peers. To construct a pack, which would facilitate inclusion in specific lessons covering all subjects and year groups, and relevant to all schools, would be an insurmountable task. Having made this judgement based on reflection on the different issues involved, the following questions arose. What do pupils themselves want when they enter the school for the first time? Do pupils want to be included in lessons as far as possible, as soon as they enter the school system, or do they feel ill equipped for such a step? It became apparent to me that I needed to access the views of pupils themselves. By accessing the insider perspectives of pupils joining the education system at secondary level I hoped to be able to reflect on some of the issues raised in relation to our present practice.

Language acquisition and inclusion

The teachers involved in accepting new arrivals from other cultures into their classes had raised the concern that learning cannot take place until pupils are fluent English-speakers. However, pupils' attitudes to second language learning and motivation are of prime importance. Language develops as a means of communication, through the need to understand and respond to other people, rather than the learning of a new language being a separate focus or end in itself. The DfES (2003) consultation document *Aiming High* adheres to the view that pupils' English language development is best served within a mainstream class context: 'There is general agreement amongst EAL specialists that pupils learn English most effectively in a mainstream situation where bilingual pupils are supported in acquiring English across the curriculum alongside English-speaking pupils' (DfES, 2003, p. 29).

Good teaching involves communication in ways which are understandable by all learners, including non-verbal language. In addition to exploring ideas and aspects of a particular subject area, it prepares the learner for 'real life' communication situations. It is generally accepted that effective language acquisition is generated by a desire to communicate rather than merely through formal teaching approaches. An understanding of these considerations is important but the perspectives of pupils are crucial, both in terms of informing future practice, and in terms of building inclusive relationships in school based on democratic principles.

Insider perspectives

Accessing pupils' views is not necessarily straightforward. Moore and Sixsmith (2000) argue that observation and non-verbal communication are important in accessing the perspectives of those who are not able to express themselves easily through the usual channels in a given context. By being able to identify with elements of an insider's perspective it is possible to develop understanding and a sense of empathy, which, in turn, help to inform our judgements and, importantly, begin to understand a situation from a different viewpoint. Pupils' voices talking about experiences when starting school are seldom heard, especially when communication is difficult. The methodology that I decided to use involved observation and informal interviews followed by reflective conversations with critical friends.

Sensitivity and care are needed throughout the process of accessing children's perspectives. The initial difficulty in gaining access to, and recording and interpreting, the views of a pupil who has very little English is obviously one of communication but there are also other underlying barriers relating to culture and trust. As an interviewer I have an interpretive role, which naturally will be influenced by my own culture, personal perspective and professional agenda. The pupil may feel frustrated that they are unable to express their feelings clearly. In the course of my work I have observed reluctance on the part of young people to speak through a third party. If the interpreter is from the same culture as the pupil the appropriateness of any criticisms made by pupils is sometimes edited during translation. This issue needs to be carefully explained to an interpreter before the interview. The pupil needs to develop a sense of trust with the adult interviewer and any interpreter present, as they may feel uncomfortable speaking frankly in what may seem to be an inappropriate way in front of an older person from their own culture.

Selecting participants

Because of some of the difficulties mentioned above, and because of the range of languages which would need to be translated, and the number of schools involved, pupils were not asked to fill in a questionnaire seeking their opinions. This approach might also have led to superficial answers. In a larger-scale research project looking at the development of inclusive practice across a school, drawing, for example, on the strategies suggested in the *Index for Inclusion* (2002), it is possible to gauge the perceptions of all those involved in a school, from pupils, teaching and ancillary staff to parents and governors. In this case the pupils with whom I am concerned are small in number and are in different schools, although the range of ages, cultures and languages is large.

To illustrate the issues raised concerning insider perspectives in the context of the overall research project, I have primarily drawn on the experiences of Dell, a pupil I know well. I have been able to observe interaction between her and her teachers and peers and also to observe how the members of the Senior Management Team (SMT) responsible for admissions have received her into school. I also sought the retrospective views of a critical friend who came to England seven years ago. The perceptions of these young people are supported by evidence from others with whose situations I have become familiar over the past three years and from teachers who have been part of their induction into the school.

An interview with Dell

Dell is a 12 year old Thai pupil with whom I had worked over a period of six months at the time of the interview. A good relationship had also developed with Mark, who had been giving Dell part-time bilingual support in the classroom over a six-week period prior to our interview. The informal interview took the form of a review of Dell's first two terms at secondary school and the information was added to existing notes of conversations and observations, which had been made since her arrival in England. I had previously discussed the idea with Dell's Head of Year as a possible way to help us improve strategies for inclusion. The school had made positive efforts to include Dell in a class that, it was thought, would provide good peer support, and this had apparently been successful. Several meetings had taken place where Dell was present either with the Head of Year and myself or with the bilingual support worker, Mark, and myself. This ensured that Dell was not alarmed by the situation of being given the opportunity to talk openly to the adults who were making decisions about her progress or daily routines. Open-ended questions were used as far as possible and the format was that of a conversation, with the use of Thai when Dell had difficulty expressing herself in English and as a means of eliciting a more detailed response. It is difficult as an adult not to lead the questions as part of a wider adult agenda and this dilemma is an element which needs careful consideration. Dell also perceives me as a 'teacher' and however relaxed our relationship our very different situations must make barriers in terms of sharing information and points of view. Barriers of experience and culture also exist between us. Dell had experienced a very formal education system in Thailand in which teachers are highly respected and do not seek the opinions of their pupils on educational matters. She was also experiencing a huge change in culture and surroundings from the tropical landscape and climate of rural Thailand to an urban landscape set in a northern English winter. These were all issues which I had to bear in mind.

During the interview Dell expressed concern primarily with the attitudes (as she perceives them) of the teacher and her peers rather than the strategies or differentiated work that would support her learning, whereas as a professional I was primarily concerned with her 'access to the curriculum' framed in possibly narrow terms relating to pedagogy. It was necessary for me to revise my professional judgement as to the priorities of her needs. Dell did see learning as a very important part of her induction period; she knew how her learning could be supported and she generally relied on peers to help with this. However, she was also frustrated and worried by this and she did not relish having to rely on others. She admitted that at first she had been a bit scared of Claire, a pupil who had been asked to 'look after' Dell when she first started at the school, and had seen herself as a burden:

DELL: I started school in January. It was very cold. I thought it was so OK. Mrs Anton said to Claire to look after me. I was scared of Claire, because all the time she make me feel she's bored at me. But now I can understand English and I not scared of Claire now. I think it hard for Claire to teach a girl who don't know English. But I still scared of Claire. I try to go away with other friends so Claire not bored.

An example of Dell's uncertainty being sensitively supported by her peer group occurred during her second week in school, when she admitted to me that the sticky yellow rice that had been given to her by her mother for lunch a couple of days earlier had flowed out of its paper bag all over her new exercise books. I helped her remove the worst of it but then was told by the form teacher that providing a new set of books would not be possible. Dell was mortified but her peer group decided that they would speak to individual subject teachers on her behalf and try to obtain a new set of books. The form teacher had been very welcoming and supportive when Dell joined the school but this lack of empathy demonstrated how little understanding there was of Dell's situation and how utterly strange every facet of life must feel to her. As time went on and I started to *listen* to Dell I began to form a clearer picture of her view of the world and the issues, difficulties and 'triumphs' which are important to her.

Support for Dell

As Thai is a rare language in the LEA we were unable to provide any bilingual support for Dell until she had been in school for a term and, as mentioned above, she relied heavily on a group of girls who had been asked to be her 'buddies'. I had spent time observing Dell and her buddy group in class and it was evident that Dell's ability to access the curriculum was largely due to the support of four girls rather than the class teachers or mainstream support staff. The girls made sure Dell had the right equipment for lessons, called for her each day and accompanied her to school. They simplified teacher instructions and gave her opportunities to practise answers before answering in front of the full class. One of the girls, Claire, was skilled at simplifying texts and explaining technical vocabulary to Dell, and it was Claire rather than the teacher who had given Dell this support during the lessons:

DELL: I [used to] follow Claire and copy her work. Now I don't copy Claire. I use my brain. I listen and ask Claire what it means. We use my machine [electronic translator] if my sister not got it. I use my brain and try hard.

The following extract from a conversation between Dell, Mark and myself illustrates the importance of the peer group and that, despite her difficulties, she felt happy about her welcome into school. It also shows that Dell recognises the need for bilingual support and differentiated work. She understands that she is really only just beginning to get the gist of the content of lessons:

M.C.: Have your friends helped you?
DELL: Yes, good friends . . . Claire, Alice, Sonia and Linda. They help me, and my Mum happy because I got friends. . . . I like school in England better. When I came England I can't speak English. Now I can. I understand a little bit in lessons. In History we had to do about six wife of Henry VIII. I got an A!

M.C.: Well done! Your English is getting very good now. How could we have made it easier for you when you first started school in England? [Question translated into Thai by Mark]

DELL: Having Mark help me.

MARK: I speak less and less Thai to Dell now. . . . At first I spoke Thai with her all the time. I think she was relieved to have a proper conversation with someone. I had to translate more for her. It would have been useful to have had lesson planning and key vocabulary in advance.

The issue of ensuring that Dell had key vocabulary in advance so that she had time to familiarise herself with the words and understand their meaning was a constant battle with some members of staff. Observation and discussions suggest that the differentiation of tasks and the pre-teaching of technical vocabulary were not perceived by some teachers as part of their role.

Dell had progressed very well in the development of her English language and was able to communicate some of her ideas and ask questions, but it was evident from classroom observations that she was getting very little support from staff. In one lesson it was apparent that she had been given neither a textbook nor an exercise book to use in the lessons that she attended during her first term in school. When this was queried the teacher claimed that she was waiting for Dell to learn English so that she could start teaching her the subject. Dell was able to understand the required geographical task about using co-ordinates to retrieve information from maps, without assistance. It seemed that no credit was given to Dell's prior knowledge and understanding. This was also illustrated later in the summer term when Dell had a poor result in her Science test. After discussion with Mark it was felt that this was not a true reflection of Dell's ability in Science and that she should not be moved from the top to the lowest Science set as was proposed by her Science teacher. It was arranged that Mark would translate the test into Thai and the outcome would then be part of the review of Dell's placement in a Science set. Dell's consequent high level of performance in the translated test changed the attitude of the Science teacher towards her.

M.C.: How did Dell get on with the Science test you were going to translate?

MARK: Excellent, and it proved a point to Mr P. He recognises that she is there now. Some teachers don't.

DELL: I could not understand the science test. I can do the work but I can't understand the question wanting me to do.

M.C.: What about the teachers?

DELL: Not everybody helpful. Some teachers do not speak to me. Sometimes they can't understand me, so they don't speak to me. I tried to talk to them but I am shy . . . in Science we get key words and he explain to me now, not before. Nobody others do that.

Dell's experiences and her own determination to succeed have been instrumental in proving her abilities are greater than might be suggested by her
level of attainment in English. Greater guidance needs to be given to staff
who have not worked with new arrivals and are unsure how to overcome
the barriers to learning encountered by pupils such as Dell. This seems to
be an issue of some contention, as schools feel overburdened with staff meetings already. The offer of an extra meeting to give training at short notice
was met with reluctance by Dell's secondary school, as meeting agendas are
set well in advance. However, training to increase teachers' knowledge and
confidence is a priority area of policy and guidance, which needs addressing
thoroughly. As teachers we must not only develop good practice but must
also be aware that the individual child has a human right to education and
this must be fulfilled. The duty to do this is clearly set out in the inclusion statement of the National Curriculum and is quoted in the document
Respect for All:

> The inclusion statement in the National Curriculum for England
> describes schools' responsibility to provide a curriculum that meets the
> specific needs of individuals and groups of pupils. The statement
> provides examples of how this responsibility can be met. It sets out
> three principles that are essential for teachers and schools to follow
> when developing an inclusive curriculum:
> - setting suitable learning challenges;
> - responding to pupils' diverse learning needs;
> - overcoming potential barriers to learning and assessment for indi-
>   viduals and groups of pupils.
>
> (QCA, 2002)

The statement not only defines schools' responsibility to groups of pupils
but also to the specific needs of individuals. This does not always require
additional time or funding but does require an empathetic attitude and a
commitment to developing inclusive practices.

Adult reflections on childhood experiences

After reflecting on the experiences of Dell and others and the issues which
are of prime and immediate importance to them, I wondered whether perceptions of the importance of educational experiences change with time. As
students become more familiar with the systems and expectations of society,
do the aspects which caused anxiety at an earlier time fade into insignifi-
cance? I asked Alo, a 19 year old Nigerian Law student, to act as a critical
friend. She shared her experiences of coming to England in the 1990s at
the age of 12, and reflected on whether she felt that her perceptions had
changed as she had matured and had become more familiar with life in

England. Alo had spoken about her memories of starting school in England, some of which had horrified me personally and as a 'professional', but those aspects were not the ones which seemed high on Alo's agenda. For example, on her first day her form teacher had declared that her name Abialo was far too difficult to contemplate using in school so she should make a choice to be either known in school as 'Abi' or 'Alo'. She chose the second syllable of her name. Alo said that her mother was angered by this meaningless choice but Alo did not see it as particularly important.

Alo's sense of identity is linked closely with her African heritage and this was the part of her life which caused her to fight her way through the early days of school in England.

> My first few days of school in the UK were extremely 'temperamental', to say the least. I got into many fights, usually because of things people had said to me about being from Africa. The perception that being from a 'Third World' country made me in some way stupid or incapable of comprehension greatly annoyed, as well as dismayed, me. I thought it was wrong for people to think any less of me because I was foreign, but I couldn't make them understand that, so unfortunately I thought I'd knock some sense into them – literally!
>
> (Abialo, 2002)

Later she realised that the actions of her fellow students were because of 'childish ignorance' and had managed to depersonalise the experience. Her perceptions had mellowed over time but she did recognise that her experiences were to some extent instrumental in her present attitude towards people.

Perceptions of race and ethnicity

Race and ethnicity of different groups are perceived differently; some stereotypical perceptions are more 'positive' than others. Alo expressed the view that her African heritage gave her the perceived stereotype of stupidity. In contrast, Dell's Thai ethnicity identified her, for some, with a stereotype of sweetness and a 'doll-like' quality by a teacher at her school: 'She's no trouble and I am sure she won't be . . . Thai people are OK, aren't they? They don't cause trouble. She looks bright . . . a pretty little girl.'

Hamid, on the other hand, as an 11 year old Albanian Kosovan, was initially seen as a European and therefore 'like one of us' by the white pupils in his school but was treated with suspicion by some fellow Muslim pupils and rejected as not being a 'proper Muslim'. His friendly character, quick mind and enviable football skills soon earned him the respect of all his peers. This respect was later put under strain when his father was detained in prison after the failure of his appeal for refugee status, a situation compounded by negative reporting about asylum seekers in the press. Hamid then became seen as a boy from a criminal family who were part of the 'Eastern European drift' to the West of 'scroungers' and, like Alo, initially felt the only way to counteract the bullies was to fight back. He was then well supported by his school, which acted to address the issue with his peers.

The different perceptions of, and behaviour towards, particular groups can make a great deal of difference to the experiences of pupils joining UK schools, as can be seen in Floella Benjamin's autobiography *Coming to England*:

> One day the teacher who took us for English asked me to read a passage from a book, so I stood up and read in my most lyrical Trinidadian accent – but in mid-flow she shouted, 'Stop, you guttersnipe. If you want to stay in my class and be understood by everyone you will learn to speak the Queen's English.' I was devastated. I started to cry, not because she called me a guttersnipe – she called everyone that – but because I was being stripped of my identity in front of the whole class. . . .
>
> (Benjamin, 1995, p. 79)

The suppression of cultural identity and devaluing of heritage language precludes true inclusion – if you cannot celebrate your whole self and feel it is valued and respected within the school or workplace, how can you feel fully included by that institution?

The pupils we are aiming to support are often at a very vulnerable point when their sense of cultural identity is challenged. None of the pupils in this study had any choice about leaving their homes and moving to England. All of them identified strongly and positively with their 'home' culture regardless of the circumstances which caused them to leave. For example, Hamid observed:

> In Kosova the books were much thicker than this. The books were more difficult and we read a big, thick book every day. We worked much harder in school.
>
> (Hamid – while reading a text during the
> Literacy Hour, Year 6 KS2)

Attitudes, support and the link with inclusion

How pupils' status and ethnicity are perceived, and how pupils themselves perceive the attitudes of their peers and teachers, are crucial factors in the successful inclusion of pupils into school life. I witnessed an example of this difference when the three younger members of a family seeking asylum were quickly and happily settled into a primary school. The children spoke no English but were welcomed by staff and peers. They progressed rapidly and soon began to learn essential phases for everyday classroom communication. Their elder brothers, who understood and spoke a little English, had a different experience. Their designated secondary school was unwilling to admit them without checking the legality of their right to education in the United Kingdom and the provision of a bilingual Classroom Support Assistant. No bilingual support was available in their particular language at the time, consequently the two boys started half a term later than their younger siblings. A full staff meeting was called and LEA representatives were asked to answer staff concerns. The boys were deemed by some staff to be a 'Health and Safety issue' on the grounds, they argued, that they would not be able to tell staff when they needed to visit the toilet. Happily once admitted the other pupils in their class and members of staff made them very welcome.

This again affirms how the support of fellow pupils and a positive and open attitude on the part of staff are crucial to the successful admission and inclusion of all pupils. Being accepted socially within a group and feeling included by that group is necessary before learning can take place in the classroom. Alo had a difficult experience with some other pupils and staff but Dell was welcomed and owes much of her rapid progress in English language development to fellow students rather than the 'provision' available. Although the initial perception of the school is that it is 'welcoming', there is still a need for a considerable cultural shift in terms of attitudes and practices at all levels of the school organisation.

Discussion: how will pupils' views affect policy?

In this chapter I have discussed some of the practical and attitudinal difficulties relating to inclusion experienced by pupils, schools and local authorities which have serious implications for children's rights. The pupils interviewed want to be included and accepted by their peers and teachers and they want to participate fully in the school community. They don't want to be perceived as outsiders, and the need to listen to the pupil's voice is paramount in making changes to policy, culture and practice. Gillborn and Youdell (2000) recognise that solutions which work towards removing inequalities need to be addressed on the macro-level, through legislation, policy and guidance, but also on the micro-level, as individuals, both staff and pupils, can make significant differences to young people's lives. Participatory action research is very much concerned with the reality of what actually happens in an organisation and how the interactions and values of people there impact upon their day-to-day activities and relationships. As Gilborn and Youdell note, 'an individual teacher can make an enormous difference to the lives of hundreds of young people' (2000, p. 221). It is at this micro-level that by listening to the insider perspective of pupils and teachers we recognise the need to make radical changes in cultural practices in schools, not only with reference to pupils such as those who have contributed to this project, but to school communities as a whole. We need to develop a *listening* culture in which the views of all members are considered important in bringing about change.

Schools in the authority who exhibit the 'least exclusive' practices in relation to pupils arriving from other cultures are often those who are supported by EMAG funding and who have specialist additional EMA staff, but not exclusively. In general it is those schools with an empathetic approach to *all* pupils, recognising that social acceptance and inclusive participation are essential contributory factors in the learning experience. The Ofsted report *Evaluating Educational Inclusion* emphasises the need to identify, monitor and evaluate pupils' needs and progress, and for practical and sensitive steps to be taken in order to meet the individual needs of pupils:

> An educationally inclusive school is one in which the teaching and learning, achievements, attitudes and well-being of every young person matter. . . . This does not mean treating all pupils in the same way. Rather it involves taking account of pupils' varied life experiences and needs.
>
> (Ofsted, 2000, p. 7)

One of the issues which must be reflected in policy and guidance is to ensure that teachers see each pupil as having an equal right to education, and in order to support that, the amount of time given specifically to each pupil may not be equal. The question of how the 'right' is understood is not always answered in ways which recognise individual differences.

In seeking the insider perspectives of the pupils as part of a wider project, some common threads emerge. The importance of the peer group is paramount. This confirms the professional opinion in our LEA that the first priority for the successful welcoming of pupils into school is to establish a supportive peer network. The stereotypes and possibly negative perceptions teachers have of pupils must be challenged and account must be taken of the previous experiences and prior knowledge of pupils. However, I found the most powerful elements in this project are the voices of the pupils themselves. They demonstrate a clear understanding of the difficulties faced by schools and by themselves and willingness to work hard to overcome them. As teachers we must respect their opinions and facilitate their right to education. As one 13 year old African boy commented to me, 'We like to talk and we like someone to listen.'

References

Benjamin, F. (1995) *Coming to England*, London: Pavilion Books.
Booth, T. (2003) 'Inclusion and exclusion in the city: concepts and contexts', in P. Potts (ed.) *Inclusion in the City*, London: Routledge Falmer.

Booth, T., Ainscow, M., Black-Hawkins, K., Vaughan, M. and Shaw, L. (2002) *Index for Inclusion*, Bristol: Centre for Studies on Inclusive Education.

DfES (2003) *Aiming High: Raising the Achievement of Minority Ethnic Pupils*, London: Department of Education and Skills (ref: DfES/0183/2003).

Gillborn, D. and Youdell, D. (2000) *Rationing Education: Policy, Practice, Reform and Equity,* Buckingham: Open University Press.

Henry, C. and Kemmis, S. (1985) 'A point-by-point to action research for teachers', *Australian Administrator* 6 (4), 1–4, cited in B. Atweh, S. Kemmis and P. Weeks (eds) *Action Research in Practice,* London and New York: Routledge.

Moore, M. and Sixsmith, J. (2000) 'Accessing children's insider perspectives', in M. Moore (ed.) *Insider Perspectives: Raising Voices, Raising Issues*, Sheffield: Philip Armstrong.

OfStEd (2000) *Evaluating Educational Inclusion,* London: OfStEd (ref: HMI 235).

QCA (2002) *Respect for all: valuing diversity and challenging racism through the curriculum,* < www.qca.org.uk/ca/inclusion/respect_for_all/index.asp>.

Chapter 7

Ordinary teachers, ordinary struggles

Including children with social and communication difficulties in everyday classroom life

Kathy Charles

This chapter focuses on the possibilities which the use of research action in the classroom can offer mainstream teachers struggling to maximise the inclusion of children experiencing difficulty in the everyday milieu of school life. The research focused on an individual child, Joe, a Year 4 pupil who was experiencing difficulty connecting with many aspects of both learning and social life. I was immersed in debates surrounding inclusive education at the time when Joe first came to my attention because I was involved in a continuing professional development course at a local university and this, together with initial engagement with the *Index for Inclusion* (Booth *et al.*, 2002) in the workplace, focused my thinking on the identification of barriers to participation for particular pupils at risk of exclusion in the learning environment. Joe was experiencing difficulties and I was aware that he would feel uncomfortable if expected to articulate his views and feelings about what was happening to him. I realised a radical approach to accessing his perspectives would be required and began to think about developing possible strategies for accessing his views. My aim was to use research action to find out more about Joe's perspective and subsequently help bring about increasingly inclusive practice in the classroom.

Researching Joe

Most teaching and support staff who knew Joe were able to offer their personal views on his difficulties and behaviour patterns. I chose, however, to harness the expertise of other children in the class to help elicit Joe's own views. I decided to supplement insights provided by other children with observation of Joe's participation in the learning environment and to build into the study a focus on planned interventions. As I was a busy classroom teacher with only limited time available to conduct what would have to be a small-scale study, I opted to focus specifically on researching Joe's involvement in only one aspect of the curriculum, the Literacy Hour. The outcomes of the project, in both enhancing access to the views of a less articulate child and facilitating interventions to increase his connection with learning, may have wider implications for the promotion of inclusive practice in other areas of the teaching and learning curriculum in mainstream schools.

Joe's difficulties and differences had been evident to teaching staff throughout his time in school and as he progressed into Key Stage 2 he was experiencing increasing difficulty in engaging with many aspects of school life. The concern expressed by his class teachers had originally centred on Joe's lack of social ease, and his apparently poor understanding of the rules of simple games, his inability to share with other children or accommodate them in his play, and his frequent tantrums when he was not able to have his own way. Joe appeared quite content with his solitary play and enjoyed the company of adults, often engaging in lengthy conversations with them, provided the topic was of his own choosing. Initially these traits were attributed to Joe not having attended a nursery or pre-school and being an only child of very attentive parents. The concern expressed by Joe's teachers at this stage focused on perceived problems and deficits associated with Joe himself, rather than with the school's own culture and practices.

As he moved through the school Joe's obvious distress, confusion and frustration with many aspects of his life in school became evident through an increase in emotional outbursts, defiance and general unhappiness. Eventually Joe's parents were persuaded to allow the school to seek advice from a variety of outside support agencies. The professional assessment identified Joe's difficulties in the area of language processing, communication and social skills frequently associated with what is described as 'autistic spectrum disorder'. Funding was made available for classroom support from an experienced Learning Support Assistant, and it was agreed that school staff could receive training to enable a more focused approach to Joe's learning.

It was during the early years of Joe's time in school that the National Literacy and Numeracy Strategies were introduced, with their prescriptive, direct, whole-class teaching content. In seeking a structure to help raise achievement, the school adopted both strategies in a fairly rigid manner and the Literacy and Numeracy Hour became a feature of each school day. The efficacy of these government-led initiatives for the teaching of pupils with special educational needs has been widely debated (Corbett, 2000; Wearmouth and Solar, 2001) and varying opinions have been expressed. For Joe, and several other pupils in the school, it quickly became apparent that this more structured teaching strategy constituted a barrier to their participation in the learning environment.

Watching Joe

During the year Joe spent in my own class I was very aware of his increasing inability to cope with these structured lessons. He found the initial section of the Literacy Hour particularly hard to cope with and, often, would not join in the shared reading or direct teaching aspects of the lesson. Although a variety of strategies were tried in an attempt to engage his attention, Joe found it impossible to focus for any length of time on the shared text or any teaching activities. He would frequently become distracted by noises outside the classroom, small pieces of fluff or dirt on the carpet or a particular phrase used by either myself or another child, which he would then repeat over and over. Joe's difficulty in understanding and following instructions created an enormous barrier to his engagement with independent tasks and he was often left sitting on the carpet while others moved to their tables.

Observation of a student teacher in Joe's class allowed me the opportunity to assess Joe's participation in the Literacy Hour in Key Stage 2. Being able to take time to stand back and watch him gave me several insights into his learning and development. Little progress was evident in his ability to engage with the teaching content of the lesson or with the specific activities involved in the Literacy Hour. Following discussion with the teaching assistant and student teacher it was decided that the Literacy Hour would be the most appropriate focus for intervention, as it was here that Joe's difficulties with engagement were most obvious.

An initial observation was conducted during a literacy lesson in which no additional adult support was available to him. I noticed that Joe joined his peers on the carpet in preparation for the shared reading section of the Literacy Hour. No social contact with other children was evident. Joe's relative isolation was very noticeable amidst the general chatter and pushing as the children took their places. Joe sat with head down, his gaze fixed on his fingers, which he drummed repeatedly on his knees. He had been allocated a specific place near the class teacher, a strategy which had been recommended in order to facilitate reminders for him to attend to the teaching activity and focus on any instructions given. On the first occasion when I observed Joe, several children became aware that he was not sitting in this allocated place and began, with increasing volume, to both inform the teacher of this and instruct Joe to move. His reaction was to remove himself from the group and sit under a table with his back to the teacher.

The activity of shared reading also created difficulties for Joe. As texts were distributed he approached the group, remaining on the periphery, and then further disruption arose due to Joe's adamant refusal to share a book with the child closest to him. Joe eventually kept the book to himself and spent the session reading a totally unrelated text and he was subsequently unable to participate in the following class discussion. In spite of prompting from the class teacher he spent this time engaged in actions such as rocking with eyes closed and tracing patterns in the carpet. This in turn impacted on his behaviour during the transition to independent tasks because Joe was unaware that other children had moved to their tables and clearly had not registered the instructions given. His attention therefore was given to lining up several pencils and counting them repeatedly until the teacher was available to give individual support and repetition of instructions. Throughout this lesson Joe's participation had been minimal and he achieved no more than to write the date and title at the top of his page, each underlined several times.

It appeared obvious, following this observation, that Joe was continuing to experience a variety of barriers to learning in the Literacy Hour. In many ways these were related to his difficulties with social interaction and receptive and expressive language, but it was evident that his learning difficulties needed to be addressed through shifting the focus away from 'what was wrong with Joe' and looking at what needed to be changed about the management of the literacy hour to make *it* 'right for Joe'. Admittedly Joe had enormous difficulties in focusing and maintaining attention, listening and processing information, and these problems constituted a major barrier to Joe's participation in both the learning and the social environment of the classroom. But additional barriers to his inclusion lay within the context of the learning environment and I wanted the research to explore these, so that some of the blocks to Joe's learning could start to be removed.

Limitations in terms of the pedagogy associated with the literacy and numeracy strategies have been mentioned previously and were a source of concern. In addition, discussion with learning support staff indicated that a further barrier might have arisen through the negative attitudes of individual class teachers Joe encountered as he transferred class each year. This view is supported by research (Avramidis *et al.*, 2000; Croll and Moses, 2000) which indicates that teacher attitude can be a major influential factor in achieving successful inclusion. Teacher attitudes may be influenced by a variety of factors, including the availability of resources, teacher skills and knowledge, or the level of exposure to pupils with differences and difficulties, and so I take the view that attitudinal barriers could be dismantled, particularly if staff gained greater understanding of Joe's own thoughts and feelings.

The ethos of the school was generally 'inclusive' but, as in any organisation, it was not always possible to account for the attitudes of individual staff members or to understand the underlying factors contributing to negative attitudes. However, what was entirely clear was that Joe frequently did not receive the support, in terms of appropriate differentiation of work or teaching, to allow him to participate fully in the ongoing learning in the classroom. In fact gaining funding to enable Joe to have the support of a Teaching Assistant for several hours each week appeared at times to enable class teachers to abdicate their responsibility for his teaching during more structured lessons, or even to allow his removal from the classroom should his behaviour become disruptive. Joe was present in the classroom but was not fully included in either teaching activities or social interactions. I began to question whether the presence of teaching support, or the nature of the support given, had unintentionally become a further barrier to his participation.

Having identified these potential barriers to Joe's learning, a need to bring about a degree of change in his learning environment was clear. I was increasingly developing a sense of the importance of accessing Joe's own views. It seemed to me that the perspectives of children at risk of becoming marginalised within schools need to be explored, and teachers working with them need to develop their own strategies for enabling such children to voice their feelings, opinions and frustrations. The issue of giving voice to disabled or marginalised individuals has been widely discussed (Barton, 1997; French and Swain, 2000) and, whilst being aware that the perspectives of children at the margins of school life may be difficult to access, the views of these children are often those which most urgently need to be voiced, as Moore and Sixsmith (2000, p. 149) acknowledge: 'The more negative a child's experience of schooling, the more gravity may need to be attached to the task of helping them to make sense of their own experience.'

Throughout the many discussions with various agencies concerning Joe's behaviour, academic achievement and personal needs I became aware that his own perspectives and opinions on the difficulties he encountered in school had not been considered in any way. Although the Learning Support Assistant assigned to support Joe had worked patiently to improve both his social skills and his inclusion into learning situations, Joe's own views on this had never been explicitly sought or used to inform planning. Again the intense presence of classroom support staff, and their determination to act as advocates for Joe, may have served to create a barrier in terms of his ability, and opportunity, to express his own perspective and ideas. This view is supported by Ainscow, who suggests (2000, p. 77) that 'the existence of support may eliminate any consideration of individual's views on how practice might be changed to meet their needs'.

We also assumed, led mainly by the attitudes and opinions of his parents, and possibly our own concepts of educational inclusion at that time, that Joe would perceive full inclusion and participation in all aspects of school life as desirable. I now know this may be an erroneous assumption according to personal accounts of school life written by those who have been assigned the label 'autistic spectrum-related difficulties' (Sainsbury, 2000; Jackson, 2002). The need to bring about change which was led by Joe's own views and preferences led me to my specific action research focus and I began to consider the most effective way of enabling Joe to express his feelings and give voice to his perspectives on his learning.

Thinking about Joe

I was drawn to the ideas of Dunn (2000), who had reported considerable success in accessing the perspectives of disabled children by involving their non-disabled siblings. In Dunn's study, the prompts of non-disabled siblings were highly effective in accessing the views of children identified as having autistic spectrum disorders. Dunn found that the siblings of children with the label of autism taking part in her study 'had strategies for facilitating easy and effective communication which completely eluded adult facilitators' (p. 101). I had also read that children who have autistic spectrum-related difficulties may have difficulty in recalling their own experience of events without a specific cue or trigger, owing to difficulties in 'personal episodic' memory (Jordan and Powell, 1995). The prompts used by children in Dunn's study proved far more successful than any adult strategies in facilitating the recall of specific events and experiences from autistic children and I began to think that involving other children as facilitators in the process of accessing Joe's views might be a sensible way to proceed.

Joe had no siblings but had been in a stable, cohesive and supportive peer group at school for around five years. Although Joe had never achieved what could be described as full social inclusion into the group, and had experienced difficulties with social interaction, his peers had been extremely tolerant and patient with his unusual behaviour patterns. Lessons such as PE were always especially distressing for Joe, particularly team games, and a group of children would often patiently try to explain rules and scoring systems to him with little effect and then tactfully ignore his resulting tantrums. Similarly children did not object if Joe were chosen to join their group for Art or Design and Technology projects, although he frequently played no constructive part in these activities but would be more likely to disrupt their work. I hoped to harness this tolerance and understanding among his peer group in order to facilitate access to Joe's perspectives and possibly assist in reducing barriers to his inclusion in the learning situation.

It had also become apparent through experience within the school, when observing the attitude of older pupils towards children with learning difficulties, that some pupils, particularly boys, have a tendency to lose this tolerant attitude towards less able peers as they move into upper junior classes. Subsequent experience as an educational psychologist has strengthened my view on this, particularly in noting the many negative social experiences, including bullying, encountered by pupils with similar difficulties to Joe's when transferring to secondary schools. Erwin (1993, p. 217) refers to friendships between non-learning disadvantaged children as he discusses the change in friendships as they mature. He comments that these 'increase in stability with age, particularly reflecting more stable interests' and that they also become 'more likely to be reciprocal'. Any friendships begun at an early age between a child with difficulties related to the autistic spectrum and their mainstream peers may be vulnerable to collapse with maturity owing to the lack of social reciprocity associated with autism and also a lack of shared interests. I hoped that involvement in supporting Joe's inclusion in school life and gaining insight into his difficulties might, in some part, reduce this fracture of peer group support as he progresses through school.

Finding out more about Joe

The situation I have described lent itself to practitioner-led action research, as there was a focus on questioning existing practices and a need to bring about change.

An advantage of the action research approach is that it allows the use of a number of methodologies for data collection (Rose and Grosvenor, 2001). However, the approach I took was unusual in positioning Joe's peers as key commentators on his experiences and enablers in terms of helping him to express his views. Drawing on Dunn's (2000) ideas and experience as an inspiration and guide, I decided to take an eclectic approach to my research design, using observations and interviews of varying levels of structure and formality. A further major advantage of my use of practitioner research in this situation was the availability of prior knowledge of both pupils and the learning context and an established rapport and familiarity with staff, parents and pupils which was particularly enabling during planning and interviews. The children accepted my presence in the classroom, perhaps on the assumption that I was there to observe not themselves but the student teacher on her final teaching practice. This enabled the approach to be one of comfortable participant observation as described by Rose and Grosvenor (2001).

In evaluating my initial observation of Joe in a literacy lesson it was apparent that Joe was experiencing several barriers to his participation in this learning situation. The reaction of his peers to his reluctance to conform to specific seating arrangements clearly caused Joe both distress and confusion, and the degree of social interaction required in sharing books demanded skills beyond his capacity. These difficulties appeared to prevent him from focusing on, or connecting with, the teaching and learning process.

Corbett (1999) refers to inclusive pedagogy as relating to 'degrees of connectedness': the individual learner being connected with the learning environment; the classroom culture being connected with all learners. Clearly Joe was not experiencing this 'connectedness' and was not therefore participating effectively in the learning experience. The next stage was to gain access to Joe's own views on the difficulties he experienced during the lesson.

Talking to Joe

To gain access to Joe's perspective on his experiences in the Literacy Hour I used an unstructured interview in two situations. First an individual interview was conducted with Joe, followed by a paired interview involving Joe and another child from the class. The consent of both pupils had been explicitly sought prior to commencing the study and further explanations of the purpose of these interviews, together with opportunity for the children to ask questions or refuse to participate, formed an introduction to the interview procedure. The issue of informed consent was difficult to rationalise with reference to Joe, owing to his receptive language difficulties. Lindsay (2000, p. 13) indicates that the need for informed consent is dependent upon the intrusiveness of the study and the level of anonymity present. As the study was not particularly intrusive in nature, requiring the pupils to participate in very little activity which could be described as outside the normal classroom routine, and full anonymity could be assured in any documentation, I felt confident to continue.

Tape-recording of the interviews was valuable in analysing this unstructured data, preserving the natural language used by both children and also the interactions that occurred during the paired interview. It was particularly enabling in preserving the prompts used by Joe's peers as a means of enhancing access to his views. The two children listened to the recordings, a source of great amusement which increased their motivation to continue their involvement in the study.

Both interviews supported the view that the level of social interaction demanded by the lesson was a major cause of distress for Joe. His main concern appeared to be his position at the front of the class and in close proximity to other children and the class teacher during shared reading. He continually repeated the phrase 'Loud, loud, loud at the front, gives me the headache.' When asked the source of the 'loudness' he was not able to explain further but went on unprompted to talk about the story he had been reading while his peers shared the appropriate text.

A paired interview with Joe and his classmate, Jack, was more successful in revealing insights into his difficulties. When the issue of 'loudness' was mentioned in relation to Joe's seating position, Jack's reference to the other children shouting at Joe prompted him to reply: 'They do shout at me but at the front it is Miss Evan's voice that is very too loud and makes me not think.' A comment from Jack to Joe, 'You wouldn't be reading with us anyway, would you? You was on the wrong page most times . . . and the wrong story even,' highlighted the dilemma and confusion Joe experiences in needing support in self-organisation, but being unwilling to commit himself to the social interaction involved in sharing a book or asking for help.

More structured interviews aimed at gaining the views of the class teacher and Learning Support Assistant on the difficulties encountered by Joe during literacy lessons reinforced those which emerged during the initial observations and discussions with children. Staff observations on Joe's behaviour included mention of frequent episodes of 'stubbornness' and refusal to accept adult direction or support. They also referred to his tendency to disrupt other children both intentionally, through his behaviour, and unintentionally, through his own sensory distractions. These views were supported by the detailed descriptions of Joe's behaviour in class given by Jack. An issue which arose during these interviews was the sense of frustration that Joe experienced as a result of his inability to connect with his learning environment and the explicit requirement for social interaction in the classroom situation.

In response to evidence collected during interviews and observations, various simple interventions were planned in an attempt to evoke a change in Joe's engagement during literacy lessons. These focused on a reduction of sensory stimulation, less necessity for social interaction and support with self-organisational skills. Joe's designated position during 'carpet time' was changed in order to allow him personal space and preferred distance from sounds which he found loud or disturbing while still remaining in view of the class teacher. Sufficient classroom resources, such as books, were made available so that Joe did not have to share with another child.

The awareness and insight into Joe's difficulties demonstrated by his classmate Jack, together with Joe's responses to his prompts during interview, suggested the possibility of Jack's further involvement in collaboration. Having discussed this with Jack and his parents and obtained their agreement, Jack was to be responsible for reminding Joe of his seating position, and to check his page occasionally during 'shared reading' to prevent Joe from losing his place. Peer guidance was also introduced at the start of individual tasks. Jack was to check that Joe had the resources necessary and that he had some idea of the content of the task. He was not expected to support Joe in any formal way, but to inform the class teacher of any apparent problems in order that she could then intervene when appropriate.

However, awareness of the responsibility and demands which this might place upon an individual pupil (Erwin, 1993) led me to restrict Jack's role to two literacy lessons per week. These strategies were discussed with pupils, as well as the class teacher and Learning Support Assistant. One week was allowed for the interventions to be practised before any further observation or interview occurred. The class teacher was asked to keep brief informal notes on any changes noted in Joe's behaviour and participation during literacy lessons and also on any apparent changes in social interaction between Joe and his peers.

A post-intervention observation began well as Jack led Joe to his place on the carpet and reminded him to 'listen well' and, in spite of Joe's engagement in rocking with hands covering his ears and throwing down his copy of the book, Jack persisted, found the correct page for him and Joe began to read animatedly. He volunteered to read aloud during a role-play activity and the class applauded him, causing him to cover his ears, turn his back on the class and participate no further in the activity. Joe was then unable to cope with transition to independent tasks and remained on the carpet as others moved to their tables. Jack returned to Joe, pulled his sleeve and pointed to his table. He then watched from a distance as Joe picked up his pencil and copied down the date and title. This appeared to indicate to him that Joe had begun the task, and he quickly settled to his own work, making no further contact during the remainder of the lesson.

An individual interview with Joe following this lesson was completely unsuccessful in encouraging him to disclose any views or feelings. It was difficult to elicit relevant responses without the use of overt prompts or closed questions, supporting the view of Dunn (2000) that without such cues questions can appear utterly confusing to an autistic child and lead to no answer at all or repetition of the interviewer's words. A less formal chat with Joe in the playground later did elicit more information. Although he was clearly happier with his changed seating, and had noticed that others had stopped shouting at him, he showed frustration at being unable to start his written work, and insight into his poor listening skills, commenting, 'I cannot listen too well and then I don't remember my work. Mrs B. (Learning Support Assistant) remembers and she tells me.'

Again a paired interview with both Joe and Jack allowed increased communication. Jack reminded Joe that he no longer fiddled with bits on the carpet now he had his own book, which prompted him into a description of the story they had been reading and his part in the role-play. This indicated that Joe had been able to connect in some part with the teaching and learning environment. Jack had also been aware of Joe's reaction to the class applauding him for reading aloud and asked why he didn't like it. Again this provided insight into Joe's aversion to loud and sudden noise, as well as lack of comprehension of classroom social interactions, as he commented, 'It makes me not think, the loud noise. I don't know why they do it.'

A subsequent interview with the student teacher revealed that she had noted several changes since these interventions. She noticed that Joe's attention to the lesson had increased now that he was not in such close proximity to herself or his peers and that he spent less time withdrawn into self-stimulatory behaviours such as rocking or 'finger drawing' on the carpet. She was aware of much greater involvement from Joe in the 'shared reading' section of the lesson when in possession of his own text. She had assumed that sharing a text as the other children did would increase Joe's perception of inclusion in the lesson and provide support in remaining on task. However, as noted earlier, the converse had been evident in that the required social interaction had rendered him completely unable to participate on any level.

Some improvement in Joe's self-organisational ability at the start of independent tasks had also been noted but the class teacher was aware that additional strategies would be necessary in order to significantly improve this aspect of his engagement with the lesson. An increase in social interaction between Joe and his peers had been noticed too. In the past the level of this had varied, being normally instigated by Joe and dependent upon his ability to connect with, or understand, the favourite game of the moment, but now it was seen that Jack and his circle of friends became more willing to include Joe in their social interactions during playtimes and at lunch.

Evaluating the changes

It was apparent from both observations and interviews with all concerned that some reduction of the barriers to Joe's learning in these specific lessons had been achieved in this relatively short period of time. However, it was also evident that it remained an ongoing process, which should be developed and modified in the light of Joe's own views and perceptions of his learning and the environment best suited to this. The importance of accessing these perspectives cannot therefore be overemphasised. For a child such as Joe, with significant difficulties in both receptive and expressive language, these views are not easily accessible and a range of strategies is needed. As Moore and Sixsmith (2000, p. 146) suggest in their discussion of vehicles for accessing children's perspectives, 'playing with children, using prompts to establish joint referencing and shared meaning, being with them, gleaning information through laughing and chatting, alongside more formal interview techniques . . .' prove invaluable as a source of information and was clearly supported in this situation.

Joe's perspectives were helpful in teaching adults involved in his learning to question some of the strategies previously advised to increase his participation in the learning environment, for example seating in close proximity to the teacher. The social and sensory difficulties associated with autistic spectrum disorder (Attwood, 1998) were in clear evidence in Joe's descriptions of his experiences during the lessons observed, and these had been misunderstood until he was positioned as a valued commentator on his own experience.

The presence of informal peer prompts during joint interviews with Joe and Jack evoked a significant increase in information on Joe's perspectives. This was accompanied by valuable insights into the views and awareness of his peers on his difficulties and behavioural differences during literacy lessons. Harnessing this apparent empathy for Joe's difficulties from his peers to enable his increased participation in the lesson also showed some success. Joe was evidently less distressed and confused by reminders from an individual child than by the sensory bombardment of several children shouting instructions to him, and responded well to Jack's directions during class transition periods. The evident increase in his social inclusion with the peer group was an unexpected but extremely positive outcome of these interventions.

Jack had been willing to participate and assist Joe in the project, but I was conscious that this placed a responsibility on him during literacy lessons. I had to ensure that, in creating a collaborative learning situation involving pupils, I did not create a barrier to the learning of the supporting child, although there was no evidence that Jack's learning was adversely affected. The involvement of other class members would be valuable in developing future collaborative relationships with Joe and this could also have a positive effect in terms of his social participation and acceptance by a more extended peer group.

The student teacher's views on her involvement in the research concerning issues related to Special Needs education and the relevance of pupil perspectives were very positive, as she felt a lack of direct input in this area during her teacher training course. This confirmed the views of Garner (2001), who refers to the paucity of teacher education, during initial teacher training, on issues relating to special educational needs and the resulting lack of skills and negative attitudes for newly qualified teachers who are expected to meet the challenges of inclusive education.

An important outcome of this project was an apparent increase in sensitivity from all staff directly involved in Joe's teaching to his individual needs and difficulties in the classroom. For teaching staff with experience in working with children such as Joe, the changes and strategies adopted may appear obvious and even simplistic, but for teachers encountering such difficulties for the first time, in the context of a busy mainstream classroom, the opportunity to reflect and discuss the challenges presented is crucial. The project provided a forum for questioning previously accepted ideas and practices and contributed favourably to changing attitudes towards Joe's inclusion in the school.

Conclusion

In this account of my research with Joe, Jack and some of my colleagues, I have tried to show that research practice can transform engagement with the project of inclusion. Dunn (2000, p. 103) explains that 'Allowing autistic children to put into their own words the confusing scenarios that litter everyday social interactions enables them (and us) to develop more meaningful strategies to facilitate their understanding and navigation of such events.'

Although the project presented in this chapter has the obvious limitations of scale, it illustrates the value of accessing the insider perspectives of individual children struggling to overcome significant barriers to their learning in the mainstream classroom environment. The assumptions of 'who knows best' with regard to the strategies and changes necessary to increase the participation of learning-disadvantaged children were also challenged, as Joe – sometimes with Jack – became able to express his views and preferences, and professionals came to realise that children frequently know best, irrespective of impairment or the labels assigned to them.

The role of other children in accessing the perspectives of children with communication difficulties is an under-researched area which may prove to make a powerful contribution in reducing barriers to inclusion in learning and social life at school. Harnessing pupil support and encouraging empathy for children experiencing difficulties in the classroom may also provide teachers with a means of gaining new perspectives on the barriers to participation created through their own classroom practices, and possibly creative alternative strategies for overcoming them.

References

Ainscow, M. (2000) 'The next step for special education', *British Journal of Special Education* 27 (2), 76–80.

Attwood, T. (1998) *Asperger's Syndrome: a Guide for Parents and Professionals*, London: Kingsley.

Avramidis, E., Bayliss, P. and Burden, R. (2000) 'A survey into mainstream teachers' attitudes towards the inclusion of children with special educational needs into the ordinary school in one local education authority', *Educational Psychology* 20 (2), 191–211.

Barton, L. (1997) 'Inclusive education and human rights', *Socialist Teacher* 65, 231–42.

Booth, T., Ainscow, M., Black-Hawkins, K., Vaughan, M. and Shaw, L. (2000) *Index for Inclusion: Developing Learning and Participation in Schools*, Bristol: Centre for Studies on Inclusive Education.

Cohen, L., Manion, L. and Morrison, K. (2000) *Research Methods in Education*, London: Routledge Falmer.

Corbett, J. (1999) 'Inclusion and exclusion: issues for debate', in A. Armstrong and L. Barton (eds) *Difference and Difficulty: Insights, Issues and Dilemmas*, Sheffield: University of Sheffield Department of Educational Studies.

Corbett, J. (2000) 'Linking theory with practice', in P. Clough and J. Corbett (eds) *Theories of Inclusive Education*, London: Paul Chapman.

Croll, P. and Moses, D. (2000) 'Ideologies and utopias: educational professionals' view of inclusion', *European Journal of Special Educational Needs* 15 (1), 1–12.

Dunn, K. (2000) 'Perspectives of non-disabled children on their disabled siblings', in M. Moore (ed.) *Insider Perspectives on Inclusion: Raising Voices, Raising Issues*, Sheffield: Philip Armstrong.

Erwin, P. (1993) *Friendship and Peer Relations in Children*, Chichester: Wiley.

French, S. and Swain, J. (2000) 'Personal perspectives on the experience of exclusion', in M. Moore (ed.) *Insider Perspectives on Inclusion: Raising Voices, Raising Issues*, Sheffield: Philip Armstrong.

Garner, P. (2001) 'Goodbye, Mr Chips: special needs, inclusive education and the deceit of initial teacher training', in T. O'Brien (ed.) *Enabling Inclusion: Blue Skies . . . Dark Clouds*, Norwich: Stationery Office.

Jackson, L. (2002) *Freaks. Geeks and Asperger's Syndrome,* London: Jessica Kingsley.

Jordan, R. and Powell, S. (1995) *Understanding and Teaching Children with Autism*, Chichester: Wiley.

Lindsay, G. (2000) 'Researching children's perspectives: ethical issues', in A. Lewis and G. Lindsay (eds) *Researching Children's Perspectives*, Buckingham: Open University Press.

Moore, M. and Sixsmith, J. (2000) 'Accessing children's insider perspectives', in M. Moore (ed.) *Insider Perspectives on Inclusion: Raising Voices, Raising Issues*, Sheffield: Philip Armstrong.

Rose, R. and Grosvenor, I. (2001) *Doing Research in Special Education: Ideas in Practice*, London: David Fulton.

Sainsbury, C. (2000) *Martian in the Playground*, London: Book Factory.

Wearmouth, J. and Solar, J. (2001) 'How inclusive is the Literacy Hour?' *British Journal of Special Education* 28 (3), 113–19.

Chapter 8

'What about me? I live here too!'

Raising voices and changing minds through participatory research

Judith Gwynn

Overview

This chapter describes a small-scale research project that set out to obtain the insider perspectives of a group of four teenagers, all described as having 'severe learning difficulties' (SLD). It builds a picture of the social aspirations of young disabled people by placing emphasis on their inclusion in research that claims to be in their interests. The project rests on a social model approach to education and disability and is underpinned by a philosophy that recognises the value and rights of all citizens (Armstrong and Barton, 1999, p. 1), including the right to be seen (Murray, 2002, p. 70) and heard (Moore and Sixsmith, 2000, p. 145; Ward, 1996). Such a philosophy challenges the paternalism of an education system in which self-acclaimed 'experts' purport to act in particular students' best interests while their policies sustain their continued separation and marginalisation (Slee, 1999, p. 123). The project on which this chapter is based represents a commitment to raising seldom heard voices and to positioning young people with the label of 'learning difficulties' as key commentators on their experience.

Disabled teenage lives

The teenagers involved in the enquiry were 17 at the time and in my Year 12 tutor group at a 'segregated school' in the north of England. I found early on in my research journey that the social aspirations of the four young disabled people I worked with on the project had much in common with those of their non-disabled peers:

SALLY: I make new friends.
SAMANTHA: I like lager.
LENNY: I get champagne.
SARA: I meet new people.

I knew, however, that whilst there is nothing extraordinary about drinking beer, meeting friends or on special occasions imbibing the odd glass of champagne, for young disabled would-be pub-goers realising their ambi-tions is easier said than done. Their voices are seldom heard in our culture and their lives rarely linked with such ordinary, lively social activities as those described above (Murray, 2002, p. 13).

When I attempted to raise young disabled people's voices through research action, the things they had to say created a milestone in the history of the school where presumptions about students' lives had been routinely taken for granted and rarely challenged. It was imperative that their insider perspectives were accessed so that their issues could inform the gap in knowledge about their aspirations that has been part of the legacy of years of oppression (Morris, 1991, p. 84). The presumptions and erroneous assump-tions that are made about young disabled people when their voices are seldom heard deny them ordinary pleasurable activities that others take for granted and one goal of the research was to contest this.

The case for insider perspectives

The principle of including the views of children and young people is long established policy (DfEE, 1998; DfES, 2001; HMSO, 1981, 1989, 1990; UNESCO, 1989). However, the official rhetoric has had little influence on the practice of bringing in the unheard voices of excluded young people with impairments. The most recent legislation, the Special Educational Needs and Disability Act (HMSO, 2001), reinforces the importance of planning for the inclusion of disabled children but has not yet been translated into practices which foreground the views of disabled children and young people.

In recent years insider perspectives have gained prominence in the fields of disability studies and inclusive education and, for many people who have been excluded, commitment to raising insider perspectives has offered a significant route forward (French and Swain, 2000). For disabled researchers (Oliver, 2000) the insider perspective often represents an antidote to a power structure that guarantees the silence of a particular group of people. Its appeal lies in the validity of the experience that is being described, since 'it is based upon direct experience of the way that power operates within the system; that is to say, those who are on the receiving end of decisions made about them and their lives' (Oliver, 2000, p. 8). When I embarked on the research, I had been aware of the considerable value of insider perspec-tives for some time both through reading (e.g. Hall, 2001; Keith, 1994, 2001; Sainsbury, 2000; Souza, 1997; Willey, 1999; Williams, 1995) and sharing stories of personal struggles with other parents of disabled children (Murray and Penman, 2000).

As well as moral arguments for seeking insider views, there are practical and economic benefits concerning the efficient use of resources. According to French and Swain (2000) research has historically concentrated on the psychological and medical needs of individuals, largely ignoring the disabling aspects of the environment. Despite good intentions there are huge gaps between perceived needs, often based on a medical model of disability, and the aspirations and requirements of individuals who encounter the lived reality of social barriers on a daily basis (Barton, 2000, p. 36). This mismatch between perceived and actual, self-defined needs represents a denial of people's right to self-determination as well as the unethical and profligate squandering of scarce resources where these are allocated by policy makers and planners without reference to the experience of those the resources are intended to benefit.

I was mindful, therefore, of considerable urgency attached to the agenda of raising the voices of young disabled people. I was also entirely confident that the perspectives of young disabled people I teach would – and should – make a powerful contribution to the debate on inclusion. A series of events unfolded that prompted me to seek direct action for change through research.

Socially cut off

I had worked at the focal school for seven years and had become aware of the historical implications of segregated schooling. The impact of segregation on students and staff was enormous (Gwynn, 2000a) and the sense of separateness and 'otherness' that had grown up is strongly evident in the school even now. Despite moves to forge closer links with other schools the majority of those working at the segregated school are hesitant about venturing into the world 'outside'.

Social opportunities for young people from this school are limited, with the result that most students experience a high degree of social exclusion. Although there is some opportunity in school time for students to get together, they have little chance of developing longer meaningful relationships or extending friendships after school hours. Families work hard at creating social opportunities, both within and beyond school, and without their efforts social opportunities for pupils would be minimal.

One of the consequences of failing to focus on the social life of disabled teenagers attending the school has been that wider issues around their adolescence and particularly issues to do with sexuality have also been neglected. 'Sex education' appears as a topic on the school curriculum in the lower school but recognition of this aspect of personal and social development is not yet embedded in the culture of the school. Staff are expected to 'respond sensitively' to sex-related incidents in the absence of proper guidelines and socially active students are often deemed 'challenging'. Leisure time is not an important focus of the school day and 'unacceptable' behaviour is rarely analysed in the context of missed social opportunities. Students' break time is more reminiscent of an infant-school day than in keeping with a post-16 department, since the 'more able' go outside to play and the 'PMLDs' (students described with the label of 'profound and multiple learning difficulties') remain inside where it is 'warm and safe'.

My frustrations with this situation and the apparent 'inertia' surrounding sexuality in young disabled people's lives were the driving forces behind the piece of research that I discuss in this chapter. As well as having a professional interest and commitment, I was motivated by personal experience. In addition to observing the denial of personal and social aspects of the lives of young people I teach, I had painfully witnessed my own son's social exclusion. His exclusion was not for reasons to do with his Down syndrome, but because of barriers to his social life. The denial of social opportunities to young people with impairments (Souza, 1997) is an infringement of their human rights (Aram, 1995, p. 10) and I hoped its significance would be signalled through a project concerned with raising students' own voices. The next stage was to find ways of accessing the insider perspectives of students on these issues.

The process of raising students' voices

In this section I sketch out the methodology and research tools that enabled me to address the aims of the project. My primary concern was to raise the voices of essentially powerless young people and I hoped that through this I would create with them a sense of empowerment. I hoped the work would confirm for the students that they can more than adequately comment on their own actions and aspirations (Brenner *et al.*, 1985) and perhaps encourage them to do so more regularly. I was interested in focusing on student relationships and investigating the importance of these relationships for the students. I wanted to carry out research *with* the students and not *on* them and so this project required a substantial re-evaluation of beliefs and preconceptions about the relative positions of non-disabled professionals and disabled students in the school hierarchy. By virtue of this emphasis, the project was challenging well entrenched unequal power relations and gave the students an unusual chance to be treated as experts and to break away from their usual inferior position in school.

The participants

I invited four young people in my tutor group, Sally, Colin, Sam and Lenny, to take part in interviews which I said would give us all an opportunity to discuss some of the issues that were important to them. Whilst at pains not to raise their hopes too much I suggested that school might use some of their ideas to make improvements for them and their friends. All four participants have a statement of 'special educational needs' and are described as having 'severe learning difficulties with additional communication difficulties'. Three of the students are particularly outgoing and make a lively contribution to the classroom.

Opportunities for learning and change

I believed the students were the most 'informed authors' of themselves (Gabel, 1999, p. 45) and their insider perspectives would provide valuable sources of information (Brenner *et al.*, 1985, p. 3) that would form a new body of knowledge. I felt that the 'catalytic authenticity' of their collective voices (Guba and Lincoln, 1994, p. 114, cited in Ballard, 1999, p. 5) would challenge taken-for-granted perceptions of their differences and social relationships and contribute to alternative ways of theorising disability (Corker and French, 1999; Morris, 1991). Disabled young people are rarely given such opportunities and sharing their insider perspectives begins to make it possible for them to re-author their lives (Corker, 1999, p. 192) by questioning our professional 'expertise' and other anomalies that exist throughout 'special education' (Oliver, 2000).

Reasons for interviewing

Views of young disabled people, like the views of many children and young people, are usually gleaned through parents, carers or professionals and not afforded a credibility of their own (Moore and Sixsmith, 2000; Goodley, 2000). Interviews offered the most direct way of finding out what the four young people were thinking (Kelly, 1985, cited in Brenner *et al.*, 1985). I hoped that direct communication with the participants would bring about the 'essential bond between research and knowledge' that Oliver (2000, p. 14) speaks about, thus ensuring some internal validity to the project and maximising its relevance for the stakeholders.

Ethical concerns and difficulties

The first ethical hurdle involved obtaining consent for participation in the study and this exposed conflicts between the values of an emancipatory research agenda and a system of 'special' education in which even adult students are expected to involve parents, carers or professionals in decision making and advice (Mason, 2000). I sought agreement to go ahead with the work from parents and senior management out of courtesy, but in obtaining written permission from the parents I was aware of the power of social conditioning to which we are all subjected. Without thinking, I failed to question the ethics (Moore and Sixsmith, 2000, p. 156) of privileging parents over students.

When I realised what I had done I reassured the young people that what they told me would be treated confidentially. I hoped this might to some extent address the imbalance of parent and professional control in their lives, which I had unintentionally just recycled (Moore and Sixsmith, 2000).

Confidentiality, however, opened up further ethical concerns and the already substantial risks attached to uncovering insider knowledge were compounded by possible disclosure of sensitive material. There are inevitable tensions between being a 'teacher' and being a 'researcher' that concern anyone trying to combine the roles – for example, there is the fine line to navigate between a teacher's duties to disclose and a researcher's commitment to managing disclosure respectfully. I hoped that willingness to be reflective together with my close relationship with the students would guide me in the event of any awkwardness but it was a risky decision to take.

Added to these ethical dilemmas was the ever-present danger of reconstruction in interview-based research. To assist communication it was necessary to be sensitive to different communication styles and adopt a number of strategies to capture the 'educative authenticity' (Ballard, 1999, p. 5) of the students' voices. I also went through some personal ambivalence over whether I was actually meddling in the students' lives by conducting this research project rather than genuinely creating opportunities for new voices to be heard. All this calls for a sophisticated understanding of the role of teacher-researcher (and for me, mother-teacher-researcher) and of the ethical limitations embedded in these identities.

Describing the interviews

I conducted the interviews in classrooms, which offered the advantage of familiar surroundings. Interviews took place over two sessions and lasted approximately forty minutes. The students preferred to work together as a focus group rather than individually and a positive spin-off from this decision was the peer support they were able to offer each other, particularly with communication.

I had 'piloted' the interview with my own teenage children but left much of what happened over to the students to maximise their control over the proceedings (Goodley, 2000). I offered suggestions for the agenda but emphasised that the research opportunity belonged to them. I had to be sensitive to the students' communication difficulties and moods, which determined the pace and style of the interview sessions, and sometimes used symbols to prompt responses and focus attention. I aimed for a natural conversational style (Brenner et al., 1985) to maintain fluency and build up trust and rapport, and tried constantly to keep an eye on whether I was overly interfering (Barton, 2000). Even so, I noted in my diary after the first interview that my voice had been too dominant and determined to lower my profile in the second round. Sally, Lenny and Sam chose 'friends' from the suggested topics but it was not a unanimous decision and Colin preferred to talk about school. We went with the majority decision but promised to talk about school later on.

The focus group worked well but most of the students initially directed their remarks to me and only Lenny acknowledged the presence of the other students by laughing or interjecting with remarks to them. However, by the end of the first session they all engaged with each other and joined in with some spontaneous singing. Their different personalities influenced the interviews: whilst Lenny assertively challenged my interpretations, Sally was more diffident, for example. Such differences defy the homogeneity (Barton, 2000) implied by educational labels, and what the students told me also heightened my understanding of their individual identities and collective experiences.

Making sense of the voices

The personal versus the label

An obsession within 'special' education, with generalisations and categories, has created a false impression of young disabled people's lives, often at odds with their experiences and wishes. Despite the apparent sameness of their lives it is important to recognise their unique context (French and Swain, 2000, p. 25) to avoid replacing one set of oppressive assumptions with another. Colin's indifference to meeting up with his friends challenged my assumptions about teenage leisure preferences considerably, for example:

JUDE: You told me who your friend is in school. Colin. Do you have any friends outside school?
COLIN: No.
JUDE: You don't?
COLIN: No.
JUDE: You know when you go home, who do you talk to?
COLIN: Mum.
JUDE: Your Mum?
COLIN: Yeh.
JUDE: And your Dad?
COLIN: Mmm.
JUDE: Aren't they your friends?
COLIN: A little bit.
JUDE: A little bit. Right. Would you like to have some friends outside school?
COLIN: No.
JUDE: You're not bothered?
COLIN: Not bothered.

Each student's description of social events has its own validity and illustrates how individuals struggle to make sense of their lives. Lenny has friends locally, for instance, whereas Sally, Sam and Colin depend largely on family or extended family for friendships, which is more usual for students in the school.

'Own experts'

The students are undoubtedly their own experts on their experience and identities (Souza, 1997, p. 13) and clearly resisted identities fashioned for them from normative concepts of ability (French and Swain, 2000). They talked confidently and openly about their lives and were prepared to challenge factual inaccuracies:

JUDE: Oh, I know Sophie, the student from our school – sometimes goes to Jenny's house. OK. And Jenny only has one son.
LENNY: No, *two* [insisting forcefully].

or incorrect names:

JUDE: Sam, you're going to tell us. What happens when you fall out with Andrew? Do you ever have rows with Andrew?
SAM: *Not* Andrew. It's Alice.

They have their own views on individual personalities and offer creative and interesting solutions to behaviour management:

LENNY: Hey, one more thing . . .
SAM: Alice always . . .
JUDE: One more thing, then. Go on, then!
SAM: Alice always . . . mm . . . fight, fight, fight, fight, fight, fight, fight, fight [. . .]
LENNY: I . . .
JUDE: I know.
LENNY: C . . . I like, I like everybody, everybody . . .
SAM: . . . every time. I get fed up with it.
JUDE: You like everybody to help each other.
SAM: And she put . . .
SALLY: Yeh, yeh, yeh.
JUDE: That's good.
SAM: She put kn-knives in people's face . . .
LENNY: You know, last night . . .
JUDE: Who did that?
SAM: Alice.
JUDE: Oh dear. And did you, did you sort that problem out?
SAM: Yeh.
SALLY: Yeh, I sort problems with Richard.
LENNY: You know, last night, last night . . . I tell you what I did at dinner, at dinner time. [Talking in the background.] I eat my dinner like that, I sit there, like that. I eat my dinner, Alice sit over there, right, Alice eats a fork, my bottle of drink in – I say, 'Gi' o'er! Stop it now!'

JUDE: Did she stop?

LENNY: No.

JUDE: What did you do?

LENNY: I got annoyed. I didn't know what to do.

JUDE: How did you solve that problem?

LENNY: Eh?

JUDE: Did you ask somebody to help you?

LENNY: Yeh.

SALLY: No, just me doing it, so . . .

JUDE: Did you help?

SALLY: Yeh. Lenny and Colin, problem up so . . .

From these exchanges it is clear that the students could advise on a variety of topics, asserting their opinions and defying assumptions that people with the 'learning difficulties' label do not have a mind of their own as Lenny illustrates with his sudden declaration we should finish. The students' perspectives cover a range of difficult concepts requiring mature reflection such as friendships and relationships. Lenny defines a good friend as 'someone who is funny' whereas Sam is more community-minded and identifies 'helping' as a positive attribute. Sally finds it hard making friends and recalls old friends whom she no longer sees and confides, 'I miss them, actually.' They also possess a capacity for abstract thought, as Lenny's explicit account of meetings with his friends and Sam's detailed directions to a friend's house demonstrate:

JUDE: You go to their houses. Do you?

SAM: Andrew's.

JUDE: You go to Andrew's house. Is that d' you . . .

LENNY: Long, long way, Andrew Stevens.

JUDE: What – from Sam's house? Is it? How often do you go to see Andrew, then, at his house?

SAM: Isn't a long way. It's down the road, near my Dad's house.

JUDE: Near Dad's house?

SAM: It's near my Dad's. Like, you turn left [gestures to show the way], that way, then you go 'cross that way.

The students articulate a strong set of friendship values endorsed by Sally's recall of the warm welcome other students showed her when she first arrived. Their particular interest, however, is in adult social pursuits, as Sally's frequent references to relationships and love indicate:

SALLY: Now become more younger teenagers in post-16 site. I'm new at school so I like dance with my boyfriends. I go out with them and . . . um . . .

LENNY: And kiss.
SALLY: And kiss and I dance and I back together again.

Such preoccupations seriously challenge the stereotypical image of the eternal child with a 'low mental age' often ascribed to people 'with learning difficulties'. In contrast, Colin still enjoys riding his pedal go-cart in the park and socialises usually with his parents, which may of course be through expediency and not choice (Mason, 2000). On the other hand, he likes to go to the pub with his parents, for 'tuna mayo sandwich and Coke'. The many contradictions in the young people's lives throw professional judgements into question and undermine the special educational spin that glosses over their individuality.

Exploding the myths: sex, booze and all that jazz

The ordinariness of the students' stories, telling of relationships, dancing, pubs, sport, parties and television soaps belies the professional interpretation of 'severe learning difficulties' that is supposed to require a separate 'special' environment to meet specific needs (Mason, 2000; Murray, 2002). The school underrates the teenagers' particular interest in friendships and most of their social needs have to rely on brief encounters. Yet the right to friendships is considered a fundamental human right and an essential part of being human. The students who were interviewed are entitled to be supported with this important aspect of their life through school. In answer to a question on whether they ever saw each other outside school, Sally recounted with pride how she once saw Richard:

JUDE: You could get back together? Do you see Richard when you're not in school?
LENNY: No.
SALLY: Yeh, I s'pose.
JUDE: Do you see him outside school?
SALLY: Yeh.
JUDE: Where?
SALLY: In the mobile.
JUDE: That's in school, though, isn't it?
SALLY: Yeh.
JUDE: When you're not in school, where do you see Richard? Do you see him at all?
SALLY: I saw him in . . . I went . . . I been school and I saw Richard.
JUDE: Where did you see him?
SALLY: In the . . . his bus.
JUDE: On his bus?
SALLY: Yeh. That [starts to giggle a bit] . . .

JUDE: Was that nice seeing . . .
SALLY: Yeh, so nice to see him, hey.
JUDE: So would you like to be able to see him outside school?
SALLY: Yeh.

Sally had indeed seen Richard on the 'special' school bus in the car park at home time. This poignant tale was a reminder of the utter social isolation that so many young disabled people endure as a result of being segregated and placed apart in the world. The students excitedly recalled friends' names but most of them referred to adults on whom they depended for social opportunities (Murray, 2002; Mason, 2000). As writers already mentioned have noted, lack of choice and social restrictions creates a disabling situation that is more restrictive than having no power to make decisions (Souza, 1997; Gwynn, 2000b). Mason (2000) contends that this separation from community and breaking of relationships is a continuation of the trend that starts at birth and for the young research participants opportunities to form serious relationships are limited and at best involve school students, at worst school staff:

SALLY [very deliberately]: *My* friend is Sally Brown.
JUDE: Yeh.
SALLY [again very deliberately]: *My* friend is Sally Brown.
JUDE: Tell me a bit about Sally, then.
SALLY [Pause]: She's lovely.
JUDE: Mmm.
SALLY: She's cute . . .
JUDE: Is Sally a student at the school?
SALLY: No. [Pause.] One of the teachers.
JUDE: Yeh. She works at the school, doesn't she?
SALLY: Yeh.
JUDE: And does she work in your class?
SALLY: Yeh. I glad . . . um . . . we go in Year 14. I'm very proud of that.

I know from my own observations that three of the students had been keen to explore their sexuality, only to be admonished by staff for inappropriate behaviour. However, at the age of 17 they had received little formal sex education and possibly little of the informal kind non-disabled children receive from peers (Aram, 1995). Two students showed a particular interest in personal relationships and whilst Sally persisted with the tale of her relationship with her new boyfriend, Lenny described his physical attraction to girls. The girls were more interested in less tangible traits such as 'helpfulness' or 'humour' and their comments suggest the students have more in common with assumptions made about people of their own gender than those made of other disabled people.

It has been difficult to adequately address the issue of sexuality at the school and requests to form a working party of staff and parents to first explore their own responses and attitudes to such an important issue, as suggested by Swain (1996), have not been met. Shakespeare (1996) equates such oversight with professional control where 'sexuality is either not a problem, because it is not an issue or is an issue, because it is seen as a problem' (p. 191). Educators frequently overlook the need for clear, accurate information and fail to address the issue of how to make appropriate support available. The main source of information for one of the girls interviewed was Sky Television.

Such reductionism is linked with the historical oppression of disabled people which I talked about at the beginning of this chapter and perpetuates images of disabled people as 'lesser beings' (Barton, 2000, p. 37) stripped of their sexuality and offered undemanding, unstimulating activities to 'take them out of themselves' (Morris, 1991).

Questions are often raised about the biological and ethical desirability of young disabled people forming sexual relationships (Morris, 1991, p. 20). This is part and parcel of the denial of sexual rights that has its roots in the eugenics movement of the 1930s when the right to life of disabled people was seriously questioned in Britain as well as in Nazi Germany (Mason, 2000). Such disabling discourse is handed down through the generations and shores up a culture in which the personal, social and sexual entitlements of people with impairments are denied (Mason, 2000; Swain, 1996; Souza, 1997).

Human rights

The insights offered by Sally, Colin, Sam and Lenny are testimony to a lack of respect and disregard for their right to decide even simple aspects of their social experience. For example, at morning break they are ushered into the yard, or if they are in the 'PMLD' category they stay in – no choice, no say. Social opportunities are determined according to the vagaries of school traditions – most teenagers choose whom to be with at break time according to personal attraction and friendships, but in the focal school who you spend your break time with is regulated by educational assessment.

Reflecting on my power as a researcher

In conducting this project I sought to raise young disabled people's voices but it was not an unproblematic process. Field notes, written after the interviews, reminded me that I sometimes went too fast; I allowed my voice to dominate, which had the unwanted effect of some students being silenced. At other times my interjections disrupted the students' thought processes and left them with inadequate time to respond, leading to acquiescence or my answering on their behalf. My well intentioned efforts to motivate and maintain a lively pace (Aspis, 1999) camouflaged my powerful position within the apparent partnership and I occasionally intruded too far. This produced an unwanted disabling effect on my students who quietly accepted my authority and their position in the hierarchy, as Aspis (1999) explains, 'it feels as if there is a "boss", and disabled people with the learning diffi-culties label are taught to respect and trust professionals and staff because they are the "boss"' (Aspis, 1999, p. 182).

I tried to correct these inequities and the second interview was better because the students took a greater lead in the increasingly vibrant discussion – introducing, for example, a consideration of consequences of inappropriate behaviour:

SAM: You have . . . mm . . . tell Jim 'bout this.
JUDE: You have to tell Jim?
SAM: Yeh.
JUDE: Who's Jim?
SALLY AND LENNY: Head teacher.

So having raised voices, and identified issues, the question I now faced was 'What is the potential for change to be brought about as a result of this enquiry?'

Implications for inclusion

Official policy extols inclusive values (DfES, 2001) but the gap will continue to widen between the rhetoric of inclusion and inclusive practice (Barton, 2000, p. 36) unless power holders become power sharers and listen to the voices of those they claim to support.

Inclusive schools

Students at this school are seen as the recipients of expert advice and not the 'experts of their own lives'. They become known by labels that deper-sonalise and dehumanise (Shakespeare, 1999; Barton, 2000) and legitimate their non-participation, isolation and exclusion but we are constantly in a state of denial about what is really happening (Slee, 2000, p. 145). Their voices frequently go unheard and most of the time they acquiesce, accepting all they are offered, including an identity that has been created by external forces (Camilleri, 1999).

However, whether through speech, gesture or behaviour the students communicate with authority and relevance, and for them life goes on (Goodley, 2000, p. 72) despite the dependence – creating restrictions placed on their lives by those who support a medical model of disability (Barton, 2000, p. 39). Their self-belief resists the culture of deficit and threatens the power base of the 'special' education model and helps break the pattern of oppression that is passed on from generation to generation.

Inclusive local education authorities?

After a damning report on 'special educational needs' in the local authority, LEA officers set out an agenda for inclusion. However, they failed to make the necessary changes to overcome 'habits and structures built up over a hundred years of segregation' that are embedded in all our schools and institutions and 'still dominate the experience' (Mason, 2000, p. 88). The experience is one of segregation and isolation, and this was told loudly and clearly by the young people I interviewed.

Nevertheless, the LEA's future planning includes capital investment in new special(ist) schools 'fit for the twenty-first century', either on existing mainstream sites or separate ones – segregated schools with a trendier disguise. In March 2003 *The Report of the Special Schools Working Group* made recommendations to guarantee 'a secure long-term future' to segregated schooling (DfES, 2003) and locally the role of 'special' schools is considered crucial for the development of inclusion. There is no compulsion on mainstream schools to develop capacity in response to a more diverse population and the LEA strategy, as 'this decade's version of integration' (Corbett and Slee, 2000, p. 134), legitimates separation and exclusion for students such as Sally, Sam, Lenny and Colin. Just a few hours spent accessing the insider perspectives of these four excluded young people provides an unequivocal imperative to seek resistance of policies, practices and philosophies which guarantee their isolation.

National developments

The SEN and Disability Act implemented in September 2002 (DfES, 2001) has the potential to improve opportunities for disabled children and young people and to strengthen their right to be educated in their local mainstream school (part 1). It also aims to outlaw discrimination on grounds of disability (part 2) and promote partnerships between relevant parties, including children and young people. Despite this important development and the welcome rhetoric from government circles that disabled people should have full enforceable civil rights, for many the experiences are different, as can be witnessed by Colin and his friends' insider perspectives, but also acknowledged by the Prime Minister himself:

> People with learning disabilities can lead full and rewarding lives as many already do. But others find themselves pushed to the margins of our society. And almost all encounter prejudice, bullying, insensitive treatment and discrimination at some time in their lives.
>
> (Blair, 2001)

He appears to recognise the damage that such discrimination causes to individual lives and the limitation of opportunities, so that 'time is spent only with family, carers or other people with learning disabilities' (Blair, 2001). However, such fine rhetoric is undermined by the promotion of 'specialist' schools – and in my opinion faith schools too – that the government is forcefully advocating (Ward, 2001). Introducing opportunities for further separation and division will only exacerbate the social division and misconceptions that arise through lack of mutual understanding and respect between different cultures.

Sally, Sam, Lenny and Colin know all about such divisions and are entitled to have their views known. Where teachers are willing to step into the researcher's role and access seldom heard voices they can be useful allies helping to bring about changes that, in this case, young disabled people prioritise.

Conclusion

Our communities are divided, with one group enjoying a feeling of 'oneness' and others separated through a sense of 'otherness'. Divisions are created by superstitions and damaging beliefs about young people's needs, abilities and entitlements. The personal perspectives of Sally, Sam, Colin and Lenny are vital to help outsiders understand and value their differences, and as we learn what it is really like for them (French and Swain, 2000, pp. 18–19) our work as professionals will ultimately become more relevant.

Sally's, Lenny's, Sam's and Colin's insider views have taught us that their friendships and human relations need to have a higher status and urge us to explore the social and sexual attitudes that dominate the school community. Their voices represent powerful instruments of change (Tagg, p. 169, in Brenner et al., 1985) and the knowledge gained from their exchanges 'provides evidence of "the personal burdens [of shame and fear] that many disabled people have to live with" and "demonstrate how the personal is indeed political"' (Linton, 1998, p. 22, cited in Corker, 1999, p. 208). They are a catalyst for responsive professionals and other allies to critically evaluate accepted practices and adopt 'different structures and ways of working' (Aspis, 1999, p. 182). This will require a break with tradition so that disabled students may be welcomed as equal partners with equal rights.

Reflection

Raising voices and finding out about student relationships was central to my research, but they also prompted me to scrutinise my own practice (Barton, 2000, p. 37). I reflected on my apparent collusion with a system that separated young people from their local communities and denied them social opportunities. I also thought about how we, as parents, collude with the gatekeepers of mainstream society in order to have our children accepted.

However, despite these doubts there was a small measure of resistance (Moore and Dunn, 1999, p. 2000) in my duplicity, for without insider status I could not have obtained the students' perspectives, which ultimately inspired the student council and which now meets monthly in Jim's office. Although it will be an uphill struggle to get their views taken seriously in a society dominated by the medical approach to disability, the council has helped restore dignity to young people whose voices have been quiet for so long.

References

Aram, K. (1995) *Sexuality and Young People with Learning Difficulties: a Booklet for Parents and Carers,* London: Special Needs Sexuality Project, Lewisham HIV Unit.

Armstrong, F. and Barton, L. (eds) (1999) *Disability, Human Rights and Education,* Buckingham: Open University Press.

Aspis, S. (1999) 'What they don't tell disabled people with learning difficulties', in M. Corker and S. French (eds) *Disability Discourse,* Buckingham: Open University Press.

Ballard, K. (ed.) (1999) *Inclusive Education: International Voices on Disability and Justice,* London: Falmer Press.

Barton, L. (2000) 'Insider perspectives, citizenship and the question of critical engagement', in M. Moore (ed.) *Insider Perspectives on Inclusion: Raising Voices, Raising Issues,* Sheffield: Philip Armstrong.

Blair, T. (2001) foreword in *Valuing People: A new Strategy for Learning Disability for the Twenty-first Century,* London: HMSO.

Brenner, M., Brown, J. and Canter, D. (eds) (1985) *The Research Interview: Uses and Approaches,* London: Academic Press.

Camilleri, J. (1999) 'Disability: a personal odyssey', *Disability and Society* 14 (6), 845–53.

Corbett. J. and Slee, R. (2000) 'An international conversation on inclusive education', in F. Armstrong, D. Armstrong and L. Barton (eds) *Inclusive Education: Policy, Contexts and Comparative Perspectives,* London: David Fulton.

Corker, M. (1999) 'New disability discourse: the principle of optimization and social change', in M. Corker and S. French (eds) *Disability Discourse,* Buckingham: Open University Press.

Corker, M. and French, S. (1999) 'Reclaiming discourse in disability studies', in M. Corker and S. French (eds) *Disability Discourse,* Buckingham: Open University Press.

DfEE (1998) *Meeting Special Educational Needs: A Programme of Action,* London: DfEE Publications.

DfES (2001) *Special Educational Needs: Code of Practice,* London: DfES Publications.

DfES (2003) *The Report of the Special Schools Working Group,* London: DfES Publications.

French, S. and Swain, J. (2000) 'Personal perspectives on the experience of exclusion', in M. Moore (ed.) *Insider Perspectives on Inclusion,* Sheffield: Philip Armstrong.

Gabel, S. (1999) 'Depressed and disabled: some discursive problems with mental illness', in M. Corker and S. French (eds) *Disability Discourse,* Buckingham: Open University Press.

Goodley, D. (2000) *Self-advocacy in the Lives of People with Learning Difficulties,* Buckingham: Open University Press.

Gwynn, J. D. (2000a) 'Being on the Inside: Policy Making at Balott School', unpublished assignment, University of Sheffield.

Gwynn, J. D. (2000b) 'Giving the Students a Voice', unpublished assignment, University of Sheffield.

Hall, K. (2001) *Asperger Syndrome, the Universe and Everything,* London: Jessica Kingsley.

Keith, L. (ed.) (1994) *Mustn't Grumble,* London: Women's Press.

Keith, L. (2001) *Take up thy Bed and Walk: Death, Disability and Cure in Classic Fiction for Girls,* London: Women's Press.

Mason, M. (2000) *Incurably Human,* London: Working Press.

Moore, M. and Dunn, K. (1999) 'Disability, human rights and education in Romania', in F. Armstrong and L. Barton (eds) *Disability, Human Rights and Education,* Buckingham: Open University Press.

Moore, M. and Sixsmith, J. (2000) 'Accessing children's insider perspectives', in M. Moore (ed.) *Insider Perspectives on Inclusion: Raising Voices, Raising Issues,* Sheffield: Philip Armstrong.

Morris, J. (1991) *Pride against Prejudice,* London: Women's Press.

Murray, P. (2002) *Hello! Are you listening? Disabled Teenagers' Experience of Access to Inclusive Leisure,* York: Joseph Rowntree Foundation.

Murray, P. and Penman, J. (eds) (2000) *Telling our own Stories: Reflections on Family Life in a Disabling World,* Sheffield: Parents with Attitude.

Oliver, M. (2000) 'Why do insider perspectives matter?' in M. Moore (ed.) *Insider Perspectives on Inclusion: Raising Voices, Raising Issues,* Sheffield: Philip Armstrong.

Sainsbury, C. (2000) *The Martian in the Playground: Understanding the Schoolchild with Asperger's Syndrome,* Bristol: Lucky Duck.

Shakespeare, T. (1996) 'Power and prejudice: issues of gender, sexuality and disability', in L. Barton (ed.) *Disability and Society: Emerging Issues and Insights,* Harlow: Longman.

Shakespeare, T. (1999) 'Art and lies? Representations of disability on film', in M. Corker and S. French (eds) *Disability Discourse,* Buckingham: Open University Press.

Slee, R. (1999) 'Special education and human rights in Australia: how do we know about disablement, and what does it mean for educators?' in F. Armstrong and L. Barton (eds) *Disability, Human Rights and Education,* Buckingham: Open University Press.

Souza, A. (1997) 'Everything you ever wanted to know about Down's syndrome, but never bothered to ask', in P. Ramachan, G. Grant and J. Borland (eds) *Empowerment in Everyday Life: Learning Disability,* London: Jessica Kingsley.

Swain, J. (1996) 'Taught helplessness? Or a say for disabled students in schools', in J. Swain, V. Finkelstein, S. French and M. Oliver (eds) *Disabling Barriers – Enabling Environments,* London: Sage.

UNESCO (1989) *United Nations Convention on the Rights of the Child,* Paris: UNESCO.

Ward, D. (2001) 'Alone and together', *Guardian*, Education Section, 18 September, pp. 2–3.

Ward, L. (1996) *Seen and Heard: Involving Disabled Children and Young People in Research and Development Projects*, York: Joseph Rowntree Foundation.

Willey, L. H. (1999) *Pretending to be Normal: Living with Asperger's Syndrome*, London: Jessica Kingsley.

Williams, D. (1995) *Somebody Somewhere*, London: Corgi.

Chapter 9

Out of the closet, into the classroom

Gay students, teachers and research action

Colin J. Slater

> Being gay, lesbian or bisexual is not a way of life; it's a part of life.
> (National Youth Agency)

This chapter is about a small action research project which I carried out while I was working for the Home and Individual Tuition Unit in a large inner city. The unit is responsible for the educational provision for students who have statements of Special Educational Needs and who are not in full-time education, usually because they have been 'permanently excluded'. These students either attend the centre where our service is based, or they are visited in their homes for two-hour teaching sessions a week, or sometimes we hold the sessions in another venue such as the local library. The centre is based at a Pupil Referral Unit (PRU). At the time when I carried out this small project, I was the only person working in the Home Tuition service. The colleagues who contributed to the research were all members of staff at the PRU.

I set out to investigate how the subject of homosexuality is approached within my own work context with the purpose of trying to ensure that, through collective reflection and action, gay issues are included sensitively and with understanding as part of a wider commitment to developing inclusive practice. I began by asking 'the participants' (my work colleagues) to answer a series of questions relating to issues of sexuality as they impinge on the curriculum and teaching and learning. Their responses were used to assist in the creation of an information pack which I later presented to them and asked for their reflections. This chapter looks at the background to the project, especially in terms of a particular group of marginalised students – gay, lesbian and bisexual teenagers – and the issues and possible exclusion in education which they face. It then goes on to describe how the research was carried out and discusses its possible impact. As a gay man and a teacher, I approached the project from a particular 'insider' perspective, having personal knowledge of the kind of exclusion gay students may experience, and the way in which this marginalisation is implicitly supported by education systems which fail to address discrimination in this area.

Background

For many young people, coming to terms with their sexuality is a daunting and all-consuming process. Understanding your sexuality is not an easy thing at any time, and it can be especially difficult for teenagers as they also struggle with the changes that occur to body and mind during adolescence.

The path to understanding one's sexual identity can be littered with potholes and obstacles, involving tensions and complex feelings. It is sign-posted with expectations put there by others to try and ensure that 'all' end up in the direction deemed by the majority to be acceptable, that being 'heterosexuality'. These heteronormative forces (Atkinson, 2002) are designed to reinforce compulsory heterosexuality (Rich, 1983; Mac an Ghaill, 1994). Society expects people to behave in certain ways. To behave in what is assumed to be a 'normal way' sexually is one of them. The institution of school, teachers, classroom and playground behaviour plays a large part in the reinforcement of this heteronormativity, in ways which have been explored in depth by Atkinson (2002) and others (see Mac an Ghaill, 1994; Epstein and Johnson, 1998; Reay, 2001; Rich, 1983).

From my reading and from my own experience, it seems to me that there is an urgent need to do a lot more work with young men and women relating to sexuality. I can only begin to imagine what it must be like to come to terms with one's heterosexuality, but I *am* familiar with the issues that will face a lot of young people as they begin to recognise and under-stand their homosexuality. An awareness of their sexual orientation brings with it the realisation that they are now members of a stigmatised minority group and that all the derogatory information that they have ever encoun-tered about lesbian and gays refers to them – personally.

These daunting revelations are further compounded by the isolation of gay, lesbian and bisexual youth. Unlike other minority groups who usually have the support of their families and communities in coming to terms with their differences – and uniqueness – the homosexual or bisexual young person usually faces this alone, as any declaration of their sexuality could lead to hostility or rejection. Schools contribute to this isolation by not fully acknowledging their gay and lesbian pupils. Little if any reference is made to homosexual issues or feelings in sex education, let alone in any other area of the curriculum. This is despite the following statement from the DfEE (2000) Sex Education and Relationship Guidance (section 1, para. 30),

> It is up to schools to make sure that the needs of all pupils are met in their programmes. Young people, whatever their developing sexu-ality, need to feel that sex and relationships education is relevant to them and sensitive to their needs. The Secretary of State is clear that teachers should be able to deal honestly and sensitively with sexual orientation, answer appropriate questions and offer support.

This marks a huge step in terms of acknowledging differences in sexuality and a commitment to recognising and including gay, lesbian and bisexual pupils. Teachers, however, have access to little formal training or centrally produced resources in this area, which leaves them poorly equipped to understand and discuss the complex issues involved. Add to this the moral, religious and homophobic objections of some teachers, and it leaves gay, lesbian and bisexual students very few people within schools that they can turn to for support.

Homophobic bullying is very common amongst the student population of schools. As Berliner observes:

> 'Gay' is probably now the most common word of abuse in the playground, and beyond, among children and teenagers, and it is used to describe anything from the not very good to absolute rubbish. It is used to describe any kind of behaviour that could be remotely categorized as homosexual, even accidental touching in a crowded corridor, or a friendly smile in the changing room.
>
> (Berliner, 2001,
> http://education.guardian.co.uk/schools/story)

This echoes a scenario which occurred in my own work setting when a student referred to a situation as being 'gay'. When asked why they used that word to describe the situation the reply was 'Because it was rubbish.' For some it is obviously a word full of negative connotations.

Berliner (2001) argues that homophobia goes largely unchecked and the reason is that schools do not know what to do about it. She raises the question:

> But why has this problem not been considered in the same way as racism and sexism? The answer is partly historical and related to section 28 of the Local Government Act 1988. This was amended during the Thatcher era to prohibit the 'promotion' of homosexuality by local authorities and the teaching in state schools of 'pretend family relations' (lesbian and gay) as equivalent to heterosexual ones. This left some teachers nervous about addressing homosexuality at all, and the ensuing vacuum allowed homophobia to flourish.

My preliminary discussions with colleagues indicated that there were still teachers within my work context who believed that Section 28 (Local Government Act 1988) prohibited them from talking to students in any way about homosexuality. It was a revelation for some to read in the information pack which I later compiled as part of the action research project the following:

The Department of the Environment Circular 12/88 states, 'Section 28 does not affect the activities of school governors nor teachers. It will not prevent the objective discussion of homosexuality in the classroom, nor the counselling of pupils concerned about their sexuality (Department of the Environment 1988). Section 28 does not apply, and never has applied, to the activities of individual schools in England.

(Department for Education statement, BBC News
Online 2000, Friday 24 March 2000)

Having clarified this issue with my colleagues, I felt that this removed at least one obstacle in my quest to ensure that sexuality was included in the curriculum as part of the wider struggle to develop inclusive education.

Inclusive education concerns *everyone*. No student should be excluded on the grounds of race, gender, sexuality, disability, class or socio-economic standing. I feel that it is important to remind ourselves that it is about all these things, and to work hard to redress the imbalance that sometimes exists when inclusion is presented as if it were concerned with 'special needs' or disability issues.

The study

The purpose of my research was to explore how issues relating to sexuality, in particular homosexuality, were approached in my own work context and to try to develop some kind of professional development which would help us address these issues together. At around the time when I was thinking about this, I was asked by colleagues, as I have been on another occasion, to work with a young man who it was felt was questioning his sexuality. One factor in their request for me to work with such young men is that I am an openly gay man and it was therefore felt by those doing the asking that I would be the best person to deal with the situation. Personally I do not have a problem with this; however, with no real guidelines and nothing in the curriculum upon which to rely, it has been a process of self-discovery in order to ascertain the best way to handle the many interesting questions and situations that have arisen while working with this latest young man.

In my discussions with colleagues and others about my handling of this subject (of course, ensuring at all times that I was not in breach of confidentiality) I encountered many varied reactions, from warm encouragement to total shock and warnings that by discussing this subject I would be placing myself in real danger, professionally. When the opportunity arose to develop a small action research project in my own work setting it was immediately obvious to me that this would be a perfect opportunity to investigate how others have handled or would handle the subject of homosexuality in their practice and try to develop some form of professional development through further collective reflection.

Participants in the study

Originally when planning this small project I thought that I would include the young man who was the original impetus for undertaking this enquiry. I decided, however, that at this stage it would not be wise to risk betraying his confidentiality. Permission would have to be sought and I felt that this would place him in danger of being identified. I still feel that it would be invaluable to get some feed back from those for whom the information pack is ultimately intended. Therefore in the next cycle – as I intend this be an ongoing action research project – I will present the pack to a group of gay, lesbian and bisexual teenagers for their comments and reflections.

The participants in the present study were my colleagues – twelve teachers and eight teaching assistants. The teaching staff consisted of eight female and four male teachers, and the teaching assistants were five females and three males. Participants represented all subject areas and included the learning mentor, two deputy Heads and the head teacher.

Method

Action research involves a cycle or spiral of events. The research is planned, carried out, observed, evaluated and reflected upon, and so the cycle continues. Kemmis and Wilkinson (1998) refer to this as 'a spiral of self-reflective cycles'. They observe that the research may not always follow this cycle so closely and that there will be overlaps, and plans will change along the way as new things come to light. The process must be flexible and the project should be designed so that it can respond to these eventualities. Success is not about whether the participants have rigidly followed these steps but it is about whether they feel that the process has made a real change in their practice (presumably, for the better!).

Action research has undergone adaptations and been the subject of very different interpretations and considerable debate and criticism, especially from the more 'scientifically' oriented researchers, who, according to Bryant (1996), saw the 'problems' of action research as lying in its inadequate theorising, and its lack of methodological control. The 'scientific' researchers had problems with what they saw as a less disciplined, less 'objective', form of research. Perhaps they felt that they were relinquishing control, as their research methods appear to be highly prescriptive (dare I say 'dictatorial') compared with action research, which is more democratic and therefore has the potential of being more 'inclusive'.

My interpretation of action research is that it requires participation, collaboration, commitment, confrontation, reflection and action on the part of those undertaking the research in their own practice. As change happens from 'within', it places the responsibility of effecting change within the collective hands of those for whom the change is intended. When applied to education it is a model which gives teachers a real opportunity to effect change from within their own practices. It can be primarily concerned with self-reflection in terms of the researcher's own values and practices, or it can involve colleagues, students, parents or the wider community as fellow researchers to effect change. Action research is empowering and, as Griffin (1992) writes, this is so because:

> Participatory research, as a form of critical enquiry, is grounded in the following assumptions: (a) it is essential to acknowledge and address power imbalances among different social groups, (b) research is political, (c) research should move beyond description to facilitate social change, (d) research should enlighten and empower the participants to develop a critical understanding of their situation and should provide the means for them to take collective action to gain greater control over their lives, and (e) this action should begin with dialogue and reflection among participants about their personal experiences.
>
> (Griffin, 1992, pp. 168–9)

The research process

When viewing the research process with the above in mind it is clear that action research is a very personal experience and that it is all about *us* and what we want. But it is also about constraints and pressures which are imposed by external forces, and so frequently involves struggle.

As Kemmis and Wilkinson (1998) explain, action research:

> is a social process, it is participatory, it is practical and collaborative, it is emancipatory, it is critical and it is recursive . . . It is a process of learning by doing – and learning with others by changing the ways they interact in a shared social world.
>
> (Kemmis and Wilkinson, 1998, pp. 23–4)

Action research is therefore a licence to change our own practice; we can identify areas of concern, plan intervention, observe, reflect, re-plan and continue in such a way as to constantly investigate and improve our practice.

I found this very exciting, as I felt that I was now equipped with the tools to bring about change in a way that is personally very appealing. To me, the notion of 'research' has always conjured up images of lots of data to wade through and men in white coats, in other words very 'scientific'. Action research allows us to do the research into our own practice, for our own practice, in a relaxed, flexible, creative and democratic way.

Inspired by the above and from reading about other people's action research work, especially a collection of research articles related to homosexuality and education presented in a book entitled, *Coming out of the Classroom Closet* (Harbeck, 1992), I set out to design and carry out an action research project.

Design of the study

This was a very small project spanning a period of six weeks. In many ways it was a pilot study in which I began to explore and understand some of the principles and possibilities of action research. The first two weeks were spent in planning and organisation, involving initial informal discussions with colleagues to gauge reactions to the proposed study and their feelings about being involved. Having sought formal permission from the head teacher to undertake my research, I formulated a series of questions based on the issues and ideas which had emerged during the informal discussions. I wanted to find out how many of my colleagues had encountered young people with sexuality issues and how they had handled the situation. I also asked a question about bullying which made the assumption, rightly or wrongly, that everyone had witnessed homophobic bullying. As it is so widespread in schools I would be surprised if no one had ever come across it. On the other hand, as a gay person perhaps I am particularly aware of this issue; it is possible that homophobic bullying goes unnoticed in schools. With hindsight, this is an issue that I might have explored in my initial informal discussions in greater depth, but it does raise questions about the way in which the personal can inform the framing of the research, especially in terms of the 'assumptions' which individual researchers bring to the research process.

My questions, which were presented in the form of a simple questionnaire, took into consideration the sensitivity of the subject for some and were therefore framed in such a way as to try to make people feel comfortable and ensure they could answer as simply and honestly as possible. The questions were:

- In your work have you encountered students who have perhaps been experiencing issues with their sexuality, if so how have these been addressed?
- How has bullying around sexuality been dealt with?
- Do you feel that sexuality should be included in the curriculum?
- If sexuality is to be included how do you feel this could be done?
- Would you feel able to discuss issues of sexuality with students?
- Would you benefit from an information pack/ unit of work on sexuality?

I presented my project to my colleagues at the staff briefing on a Monday morning and gave the questionnaires out, asking for them to be returned to me by the end of that week. I explained why I was undertaking the project (and that it was part of my work for my Master's degree in inclusive education), that it was action research and it was aimed at changing practice. I discussed the subject matter and the reasons behind choosing it. I gave an outline of how I intended to carry out the project and my expectations of everyone as participants. I explained that the questionnaires would remain anonymous and therefore people should feel free to make any comments they wished to in response to the questions. I wanted people to feel free of the constraints of political correctness, from judgement and the fear of causing offence.

I used the responses to the questionnaires and the earlier, and ongoing, informal discussions to help me in developing an information pack relating to sexuality. The pack represented 'work in progress', to which information could be added (changed, or removed) at any time, drawing on as many sources as possible. We saw it as a starting point, a springboard for further exploration, rather than as a definitive document or set of guidelines. The information provided is about, and *for*, gay, lesbian and bisexual teenagers that can be used by both teachers and students.

The pack is divided into sections: history, contacts, 'coming out', homophobic bullying, Section 28, sex and relationship education, with references to films, books and magazines. There is a real attempt to present the material in a clear, concise and accessible manner.

I presented the pack to my colleagues – the 'participants' at an informal drinks afternoon in the hope that free food and drink would encourage more participation. I asked them to complete another questionnaire and from these and informal discussions I gained some insights into their reflections about the pack. This second questionnaire consisted of the following questions:

• Do you feel the information pack would be of assistance to you in your teaching?
• What are your thoughts on the material included?
• Would you like to see anything else added?
• Do you feel that an information pack such as this should be made available to students? (Yes or no and why?)
• What material do you feel should be included specifically for students?

'Outcomes' and reflections

The informal discussions that I had with colleagues and eventual participants in the initial planning stages of the project were very encouraging. All agreed that there was a real need for issues surrounding sexuality to be included in the curriculum.

Of the twenty questionnaires given out in the first instance, only ten were returned, all with favourable responses. The small number of returns was disappointing in itself; however, what is particularly disappointing is that I had no idea how 50 per cent of the respondents felt about the proposed project or why they had failed to complete the questionnaire. I thought that the anonymous nature of the study, and my impressing upon the participants my desire for them to answer honestly, would mean that I would have received more completed questionnaires. As I could not force the issue any further I decided that I would have to forget about those questionnaires that had not been returned and reflect on those that had. This rather low return did raise questions in my mind about what some of my colleagues were really thinking about the pack, and the project as a whole, and this was a problem which remained unresolved.

An overall analysis of the returned questionnaires showed a favourable response to the notion that sexuality should be included in the curriculum. All the respondents had encountered students who had experienced issues relating to their sexuality. The majority of responses indicated that these issues were addressed by referral to others such as more senior members of staff, councillors and a gay staff member, indicating that perhaps they did not feel adequately equipped to handle the situation themselves.

One respondent, for example, was clear that they did not, when they wrote:

> Truthfully, I really don't know where to start.

The majority of respondents acknowledged that homophobic bullying exists. If it was dealt with at all, then this was done through Personal, Social and Health Education (PSHE) in the curriculum and, once again, handed over to senior management.

The major feeling is that it is not being handled adequately, which is summed up by the following comments:

> It's very ad-hoc. Not dealt with in terms of policies and rights.

> There have been some rude remarks in terms of sexual orientation and they were dealt with in a way that I would deal with kids swearing. (Unfortunately.)

> The behaviour policy is quite clear on bullying but the staff tend to ignore sexual bullying.

And is summed up by the following comment:

> I think this is very difficult.

The question of whether sexuality should be included in the curriculum was met with very positively and, in one case, 'Yes! Absolutely!'
Responses showed concern for students . . .

> Yes, Pupils need to understand how to deal with their feelings, the range of feelings they can have and dispel any stereotypes of sexuality.

... and the benefits for teachers:

> Too many kids, with too many questions that need to be addressed correctly, need to be properly prepared for such occasions.

One response highlighted the misunderstanding and residual fear that still exist in schools over Section 28:

> In the past Section 28 has always been an issue.

The only response indicating that it should not be included was the following comment:

> Not really, as once you make something an issue people will do it for one lesson and then tick it off as dealt with.

I would agree that if the issues were not taken seriously and handled sensitively on an ongoing basis then including sexuality in the curriculum is not a good option.

According to most responses, sexuality could be made part of the curriculum most appropriately through PSHE, but it should be included in other curriculum areas, particularly English, Humanities, Art and even Science. They suggested introducing it through film studies, the use of guest speakers, and poetry, as these would make it 'easier for all'.

Everyone felt they would be able to discuss issues of sexuality with students, but two people added the following cautions:

> Yes, but [we] would need to develop a deeper knowledge and understanding related to issues of sexuality.

And:

> Yes – I have [discussed issues relating to sexuality] on many occasions – however [my] knowledge of current legislation, health issues is probably rusty and needs updating.

These responses helped me to pinpoint areas to be included in the information pack and reinforced my belief that there is a need for increased knowledge and understanding of the issues.

Once again everyone agreed that they would benefit from further information on sexuality. Responses ranged from 'possibly!' through 'definitely' to:

> Yes, definitely!!

> Everyone would [benefit].

Immediately! Any information would be a great help.

Definitely, because this will broaden my knowledge on the issue.

These responses were very heartening and allowed me to go away and prepare the information pack with these reflections in mind, secure in the knowledge that it was something that was sought and would be welcomed by at least 50 per cent of my colleagues.

As mentioned earlier, I decided that I would present my information pack accompanied by drinks and nibbles in the hope that this would entice people to attend and the relaxed atmosphere would encourage discussion and reflection. I also felt that I would be better able to persuade participants to fill in the accompanying questionnaires.

Although I did not get a full staff turn-out, as I had hoped, I managed to entice fifteen out of the twenty to the event. The atmosphere was indeed relaxed and produced the hoped-for discussions and reflections. I was disappointed, however, in the hope that I would be in a better position to persuade those attending to complete the questionnaires. I ended up with six completed questionnaires out of a possible fifteen, which was indeed disappointing. In contrast, the verbal feedback that I received was very encouraging and reflected written responses that were returned.

The second set of questionnaires revealed a number of reflections. All respondents felt that the information pack would be of assistance to them in their teaching. They felt that it 'would be a useful resource', was 'very comprehensive', has 'excellent links to Web addresses' and found the 'samples of policy especially useful'. One respondent wrote that they 'would enjoy and use [it] as an aid in my teaching'. Another felt that 'training on how to deliver would be in order to alleviate any uncertainty'.

This final comment, and others made during discussions, indicate that uncertainty exists and that there is a need for further information, discussion and reflection in order to address it.

Participants had the following thoughts on the material included:

Interesting, colourful and very attractive.

Good; seems to be a mixture of things to suit different age groups.

The real-life stories of young people highlighted how difficult it can be for them.

It was interesting to read the personal stories, helped illustrate issues and how they affect people.

I was pleased to get these last two comments because it shows that participants are being made aware of how difficult these issues are for young people.

When asked what else they would like to see added to the material, two participants came up with similar answers, which were that they would like to see examples of possible questions that students might ask and examples of how to deal with them. This, once again, emphasises the uncertainty that exists for some, and reinforces the need for ongoing work in this area.

The consensus of opinion on whether the information pack should be made available to students was very positive. All felt, however, that the pack should be made smaller, not just in content but also in physical size, to make it more accessible. One respondent felt that it should not be made generally available, but suggested that it could be placed 'where it can be privately requested'.

I would hope that with further discussions and staff development this participant would feel better equipped to provide all students with access to the information.

Participants felt the following things should be included for students: 'worksheets (showing positive attitudes)', access to 'phone numbers, activities, clubs, support systems outside of the home and school'. Someone suggested 'a laminated credit card-size info card with important numbers/contacts'.

Another commented, 'I think talking openly about sexuality is the best way of working [with] young people, not showing any moral disapproval,' and this is exactly what I would like to achieve. We need to remind ourselves that, as Mole (1995) says:

> there are heterosexual, homosexual and bisexual people in all races and cultural groups although this may not always be acknowledged by people within these groups. There are heterosexists and homophobic people in all races and cultural groups. Some people use their religious faith to justify their heterosexism and homophobia.
>
> (Mole, 1995, p. 7)

The kinds of attitudes and beliefs mentioned by Mole exist within schools. However, as educators we need to put aside our personal, religious and cultural beliefs, whatever they are, and teach, free of judgement.

Conclusion

For me this project was a real journey of discovery. Having no knowledge of action research before the project, I have begun to learn a great deal about it and its value as a tool for collaborative change. It is this collaboration, along with the fact that it is participatory, practical, empowering, political, reflective and a social process that, in my opinion, makes it less scientific or clinical than centred in humanism. As an educator, and not a scientist, this is my preferred approach to research. I have enjoyed its processes of planning, action, reflection, further planning, further action and so on, in cycles of self-reflection.

The reflections gained from the questionnaires, informal discussions and comments made to me in passing, at the photocopier or on the stairs, indicate that this small action research project has been thought-provoking for participants. How much and to what extent it has affected participants' practice is difficult to tell at this stage. It has been interesting, and unexpected, to observe the effect of the research process in terms of bringing people together to focus on a difficult (and often 'taboo') set of issues. What I do know is that it has had a dramatic affect on me. As the impetus for the research sprang from what was happening within my own practice, it has enabled me to reflect upon this and to make changes. Any reservations that I may have had about the teaching of sexuality have been well and truly eliminated as a result of this project. I can now go forth armed with my information pack, and perhaps some guidance from the DfES, and secure in the knowledge that the scaremongering that surrounded Section 28 does not apply to schools. The plight of some gay, lesbian and bisexual young people is even more desperate than people may imagine, and perhaps most do not even think about this, and I am therefore resolved to do what ever I can to ensure that their needs are met and that they are fully included as part of the school community.

In this small research project, I have been able to share and engage with others in this reflection and to encourage them to reflect upon their own beliefs and practices. For this reason, I am very proud of the small project I have undertaken. As an openly gay man the subject is something that I feel very close to and passionate about. As an educator, committed to inclusion, I want to ensure that not only are all students treated fairly and equally, but that gay, lesbian and bisexual teenagers are recognised and that their needs and interests are adequately and appropriately met. We need to work towards ensuring that gay and lesbian issues are incorporated into all areas of the curriculum and address these in ways which challenge what has always been a heterosexual curriculum. Educators need to undergo professional development to open up discussion and enhance understanding in the form of workshops, courses or in-service training, to increase their knowledge of gay and lesbian issues and to develop an awareness of what it is like to live in a heterosexist and homophobic society.

This knowledge is part of what is needed for the development of inclusive school cultures, curricula and pedagogies. As Freire (1970) points out, we are concerned with developing:

> a pedagogy which must be forged *with*, not *for*, the oppressed (whether individuals or peoples) in the incessant struggle to regain their humanity. This pedagogy makes oppression and its causes objects of reflection by the oppressed, and from that reflection will come their

necessary engagement in the struggle for their liberation. And in the struggle this pedagogy will be made and remade.

(Freire, 1970, p. 30)

Even though Freire is making reference to the education of the world's oppressed classes, I feel that it can be related to what is endured by gay, lesbian and bisexual teenagers within education. I see them as being oppressed and that there is a real struggle for liberation. I also feel that what we have begun to achieve in this project is to embark on a process of change and we must keep working to ensure that it continues. I have not been able to include the voices of young gay, lesbian and bisexual students in my project, and this is something I plan to seriously address in any future work.

During the course of the project I have discussed my work with friends and colleagues in other schools and educational settings. All of them have expressed great interest in what I have been undertaking. One friend, the Head of a primary school for children identified as having Emotional and Behavioural Difficulties (EBD), has begun to use the first stages suggested in the pack with her colleagues and is keen for me to present the follow-up session. On a visit to another setting, a secondary school designated for children identified as having emotional and behavioural difficulties, the mention in passing of my project was met with great excitement from the deputy Head and a request to be included in any further developments. These examples strengthen my belief that there is a real need and a desire within the education community to learn about, and to include, sexuality in schools and the curriculum as part of a wider commitment to developing inclusive education.

References

Atkinson, E. (2002) 'Education for diversity in multisexual society: negotiating the contradictions of contemporary discourse', *Sex Education* 2, 119–32.

BBC News Online: Education (2000) *Minister: Section 28 no 'effect on schools'*, Friday, 24 March 2000, <http://news.bbc.co.uk/l/low/education>.

Berliner, W. (2001) *Guardian* Unlimited, *Gay in Silence*, Tuesday 2 October 2001, <http://education.guardian.co.uk/schools/story>.

Bryant, I. (1996) 'Action research and reflective practice', in D. Scott and R. Usher (eds) *Understanding Education Research*, London: Routledge.

DfEE (2000) Sex Education and Relationship Guidance, ref. 0116/2000, London: Department for Education and Employment.

DoE (1988) Circular 12/88, London: Department of the Environment.

Epstein, D. and Johnson, R. (1998) *Schooling Sexualities*, Buckingham: Open University Press.

Freire, P. (1970) *Pedagogy of the Oppressed*, London: Penguin Books.

Griffin, P. (1992) 'From hiding out to coming out: empowering lesbian and gay educators', in K. M. Harbeck (eds) (1992) *Coming out of the Classroom Closet*, New York: Haworth Press.

Harbeck, K. M. (1992) *Coming out of the Classroom Closet: Gay and Lesbian Students, Teachers and Curricula,* New York: Haworth Press.

Kemmis, S. and Wilkinson, M. (1998) 'Participatory action research and the study of practice', in B. Atweh, S. Kemmis and P. Weeks (eds) *Action Research in Practice,* London: Routledge.

Mac an Ghaill, M. (1994) *The Making of Men: Masculinities, Sexualities and Schooling,* Buckingham: Open University Press.

Mole, S. (1995) *Colours of the Rainbow: Exploring Issues of Sexuality and Difference,* London: Camden and Islington Health Promotion Service.

National Youth Agency (2000) *Coming Out,* Youthinformation.com, www.youthin-formation.com/infopage.

Reay, D. (2001) '"Spice Girls", "nice girls", "girlies", "tomboys": gender discourses, girls' cultures and femininities in the primary classroom', *Gender and Education* 13, 153–66.

Rich, A. (1983) *Compulsory Heterosexuality and Lesbian Existence,* London: Only Women Press.

Chapter 10

Challenging behaviour – ours, not theirs

Karen Dunn

Len Barton's opening remarks in the foreword to this book, that inclusive thinking and practice are hard work, is evidenced as the case throughout all the chapters which follow it. As an academic, working in the relatively – and I stress *relatively* – informal atmosphere of a university, I am brought back sharply, in reading the chapters of this book, to the hectic pace of a teacher's life in school or college. Tangible through the research struggles of the pages I have just finished reading are the sounds of the corridors I remember from my own teaching career, the bells ringing, the pushing, the armfuls of books being carted from one temporary classroom to the next, the dinner duties. When Simpson writing about the constraints on her research practice in Chapter 5 notes: 'Finding the time for an observation is extremely difficult. Each time this has been arranged, Michael is absent, has absconded, a supply teacher is taking the lesson or I have been put on a cover rota,' it all comes back to me – with frightening clarity – and I am moved, before making any other comment about the value of the contributions in this collection, to stand back and applaud – just as Joe's classmates did in Kathy Charles's beautifully articulated study, on a tremendously difficult job well done!

The 'hard work' of undertaking research in difficult circumstances to bring about change in organisations, or processes to advance an agenda for inclusion, requires all of the qualities which Barton describes in the foreword. Openness and honesty, passion and commitment – yes, all these – and also, and in my view, for teachers, more than this. Teaching today is no joke, and inclusion in school settings, for all the political rhetoric, remains the cause of a good deal of anxiety with the vast majority of teachers, parents and often, it seems, children and young people too. To work to advance an agenda for inclusion, in the target-driven and achievement-oriented market place that education has become, requires teachers to have high expectations of their colleagues and those they teach. It requires them to 'see' that things can be better and to trust that those around them – despite much evidence to the contrary – with a bit of help from the social model, with its emphasis on breaking down the barriers which create exclusion, can and will change their practice and improve their game.

Sorsby's work with Learning Support Assistants evidences just this. Acting on the assertion that 'inclusion is for staff as well as pupils' (Booth *et al.*, 2000) the high expectations she has of this group of staff and the dividends that pays for the learners in that context, are clearly demonstrated. Similarly, as a firm advocate of the significance of raising the voices of children in debates around inclusion in support *of* each other as well as on their own account, it is heartening to read of Kathy Charles's work with Jack and Joe – and to see the same 'high expectations' of the possibilities of inclusion credited to children as partners with each other in the process of bringing about change. Dell and her buddies, in Mary Clifton's study, inspire the same confidence and show us the critical importance of 'relationship' in developing inclusive practices.

That some of the work which this book shares emerges from the DfES Best Practice Research Programme is encouraging and testament also to what I can only imagine has been the inspired teaching of the book's editors and their colleagues – that inclusion *is* best practice. As a qualitative researcher with a 'never really got to grips with action research' hang-up – if anything could persuade me to have a closer look, then the context into which this method is placed within Armstrong and Moore's chapter is probably it. Adapting and re-forming action research in the manner which the practitioners contributing to this book have done is impressive and I particularly like the links made with emancipatory and participatory research methods in several of the chapters. Judith Gwynn's consideration of the social exclusion which disabled teenagers face by virtue of the limited social opportunities available to them in the segregated setting where they are educated comes perhaps closer than most to 'jumping ship' to emancipatory method. We get close to the research participants in this study and we can 'feel' the research happening. The writer's anger at the disabling barriers and restrictions which the teenagers she is working with face, both in terms of how their sexualities are characterised and their friendships undervalued, is palpable. In so many books on inclusion I have read, anger is 'edited' out, almost as if we have 'done' anger – and I for one am pleased to see it is firmly 'in' this collection of pieces.

Working with Hannah to tackle a college's funding strategy not working to the best advantage of disabled students, Thompson is particularly insightful into the problems and possible limitations of action research – which are useful to raise in the context of keeping our own expectations of the methods we need to employ in researching inclusion issues high. Influenced by Carr's writing (1995) she notes in this chapter that whilst action research has many advantages, what it is for and where it is going require further interrogation. For Thompson, whilst changing overt processes – like funding application systems – might be possible with the help of action research methods, making changes in more subtle, interpersonal aspects of processes (such as the attitudes of key gatekeepers) is more problematic. Action research needs to develop to provide mechanisms for these 'soft' process issues to be assertively addressed. In my own work I am involved in developing the Process Evaluation Method (PEM) (Dunn and Moore, 2003), which places emphasis on enabling discursive and open dialogue on informal, covert and contested issues which often militate against developing inclusive practice. It seems many of the tensions around action research which the practitioner-researchers raise in this collection could be explored further by engagement with this approach.

As the contributors to this book have shown, it is important to make sure all our research practice is characterised by commitment to developing *meaningful* collaborations, to working *alongside* agencies and services, to *applying practically oriented findings*. Research which takes place outside the 'ivory tower' world of academia can pick up on a real understanding of, and commitment to, the struggle against exclusion. Research action conducted by teachers and other practitioners effects a gradual 'step change' and offers a crucial opportunity for future change and development. In the field of inclusive education we are at a particularly important juncture in relation to shifts in policy direction towards consulting and maximising opportunities for children and young people to participate in policy development and implementation which impacts on their lives. As contributors to this book have shown, children and young people often have insider perspectives which are overlooked by service providers in planning, delivery and evaluation which hold great potential to help services reach their most vulnerable contemporaries (Murray, 2002; Dunn, 2001; Moore, 2000).

I have enjoyed this book for the breadth of its definition of inclusive practices and issues. Colin Slater's chapter on the inclusion of gay, lesbian and bisexual pupils – and the issues this can involve – reminded me of the vastness of the project we are all a part of. The common usage of 'gay' as a term of abuse in schools infuriates me on a weekly basis as I hear reports of this and that activity and argument from my own 11 year old boy's school life. I have – like you, perhaps – had my rant about it at parents' evening, and shared the annoyance of it with some teaching staff and some parents, but that there are others in both groups who look dismally at you when you raise it – as if you are really 'just looking for something to moan about now' – is enough to stem any complacency. The project of inclusion is a huge one. There is evidently a major place for working at the micro-level of policy interpretation and practice to bring about change.

Finally, I would congratulate the authors and the editors for undertaking and including work originating in the 'special' sector in this collection. I read with interest Pauline Zelaieta's study of the issues she faced as the leader of an inclusion team in a special school, and the discussion aired helps me to conceptualise and appreciate the commitment of those working in that area of provision in ways I am unfamiliar with and unpractised in doing. Zelaieta's work shows that constructing and agreeing in partnership a workable, realistic agenda for research and change will add value to practice as it unravels.

Challenging the prejudices and behaviours we have in relation to each other is – after all – the business of those involved in the project of inclusion. The struggles of the participants and authors contained within the preceding pages evidence their own commitment to challenging their own learning and working practices and assumptions. As a reader I am left with a sense of deep gratitude to all of them for helping to make schools and colleges more inclusive places to be.

References

Booth, T., Ainscow, M., Black-Hawkins, K., Vaughan, M. and Shaw, L. (2000) *Index for Inclusion*, Manchester: Centre for Studies on Inclusive Education.

Carr, W. (1995) *For Education: Towards Critical Educational Enquiry*, Oxford: Oxford University Press.

Dunn, K. (2001) *Child Development and Education: New Voices, Different Experiences*, Sheffield: Philip Armstrong.

Dunn, K. and Moore, M. (2003) *The Process Evaluation Method: Inclusive Research for Change*, Sheffield: Inclusion, Childhood and Education Publications.

Moore, M. (ed.) (2000) *Insider Perspectives on Inclusion: Raising Voices, Raising Issues*, Sheffield: Philip Armstrong.

Murray, P. (2002) *Hello! Are you Listening? Young Disabled People's Views on Leisure*, York: Joseph Rowntree Foundation.

Action research spiral

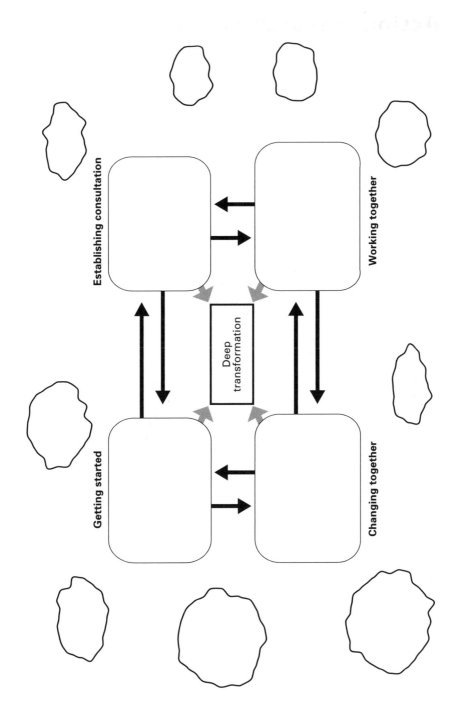

Index

eBooks – at www.eBookstore.tandf.co.uk

A library at your fingertips!

eBooks are electronic versions of printed books. You can store them on your PC/laptop or browse them online.

They have advantages for anyone needing rapid access to a wide variety of published, copyright information.

eBooks can help your research by enabling you to bookmark chapters, annotate text and use instant searches to find specific words or phrases. Several eBook files would fit on even a small laptop or PDA.

NEW: Save money by eSubscribing: cheap, online access to any eBook for as long as you need it.

Annual subscription packages

We now offer special low-cost bulk subscriptions to packages of eBooks in certain subject areas. These are available to libraries or to individuals.

For more information please contact webmaster.ebooks@tandf.co.uk

We're continually developing the eBook concept, so keep up to date by visiting the website.

www.eBookstore.tandf.co.uk